pp- 162-163.

THE GOD-ORDAINED WAY TO PRACTICE THE NEW TESTAMENT ECONOMY

WITNESS LEE

Living Stream Ministry
Anaheim, California

©1987 Witness Lee

First Edition, 6,250 copies. September 1987.

Library of Congress Catalog
Card Number: 87-82878

ISBN 0-87083-325-1 (hardcover)
ISBN 0-87083-326-X (softcover)

Published by

Living Stream Ministry
1853 W. Ball Road, P. O. Box 2121
Anaheim, CA 92804 U.S.A.

Printed in the United States of America

CONTENTS

Title	Page
Preface	5
1 The Divine Economy	7
2 The Divine Trinity's Operation	17
3 The Deformed and Degraded Christianity	25
4 The Sequence of the Divine Revelation in the First Eight Books of the New Testament	37
5 The Christian Gathering	47
6 The Support of the Church Meetings	57
7 The Basic Factors for the Christian Meetings (1)	67
8 The Basic Factors for the Christian Meetings (2)	75
9 The Basic Factors for the Christian Meetings (3)	85
10 God's Ordained Way to Spread the Gospel	93
11 The Destiny of the Branches of the Divine Trinity's Organism	99
12 Setting Up Home Meetings	105
13 The Way to Build Up Home Meetings	113
14 The Standard of Home Meetings	123
15 Absolute for God's Ordained Way	131

16	One Way for One Goal	139
17	The Apostles' Teaching and Fellowship	149
18	The New Testament Ministry and Ministers	159
19	The Leadership in the New Testament Ministry and Among the New Testament Ministers	167

PREFACE

This book is composed of messages given by Brother Witness Lee in the 1987 Summer Training in Anaheim, California.

Chapter One

THE DIVINE ECONOMY

Scripture Reading: Eph. 3:6-11

The contents of our fellowship in this book will be to study the new way for the Lord's new move. Our desire is to see and enter into the God-ordained way to practice the New Testament economy. Related to this practice, there are two crucial items. The first item is that we go out to visit people in their homes. We are not merely going to knock on people's doors, but we are going to visit people in the same way that the Lord Jesus did. He came far away from the heavens to this earth to visit people, so He also gives us the order or commandment to go to visit people (Matt. 28:19; Luke 10:3). Because we are going to visit people in their homes, we need to knock on their doors. The second thing we have to do in the new way is to set up home meetings with the ones we have just baptized. Two words are very crucial in the new way for the Lord's new move: go and home. We go to visit people in their homes, and we set up home meetings with them. We need to go to people's homes and bring the meetings to them.

All of us need to dream about the new way for the Lord's new move so that God's New Testament economy can be carried out and practiced. We need to learn to dream for the Lord Jesus. The Lord's new way is a dream that we all need to be brought into. I have been dreaming this dream, and my burden is to bring you into this dream. We all have to bear the responsibility and the burden to bring this dream to the whole earth. If we are faithful by the Lord's mercy to practice the New Testament economy according to the God-ordained way, we will see the fulfillment of this dream.

In order for us to practice the New Testament economy, we need to see the divine economy. This economy is clearly revealed in the holy Word (1 Tim. 1:4; Eph. 1:10; 3:9; Col. 1:25; 1 Cor. 9:17). The center of the entire New Testament is God's divine economy. God's economy is God's plan, His divine arrangement, to dispense Himself into His chosen people. Our going out to visit people by knocking on their doors is for this economy and should be linked with the divine economy. Since the Lord brought me to the United States in the early sixties, every message I have given has touched this point of God's economy. I was sent to the United States by being linked to this economy, and I did not do anything that was independent of this economy.

When we go out, we must hold on to the concept and deep feeling that we are going out to visit people for God's economy. Without knocking on people's doors, it would be hard for us to seek the sons of peace for God's eternal economy (Luke 10:3-6). God's eternal economy involves and includes millions of sons of peace. These sons of peace need us to go to visit them in their homes. We go to knock on people's doors by having ourselves linked to the divine economy, linked to eternity, linked to the heavenlies. We need a clear vision and deep impression concerning God's economy, which involves the completion of Christ and the propagation of the pneumatic Christ for the producing of the church (Eph. 3:6-11).

THE COMPLETION OF CHRIST

We need to ask the Lord to grant us a vision of the completion of Christ. Some may ask, "Does Christ need to be completed? Isn't He perfect?" In answering such a question, we have to differentiate between what it is to be completed and what it is to be perfected. We human beings all need to be perfected, but God's Christ is eternally perfect. He does not need any perfection. Such an eternally perfect Christ, however, needs a completion. To help us understand this, I would ask, "Before Christ was incarnated, did He have the human nature?" Concerning this matter of having the human nature, He needed to be completed. Before Christ was incarnated, He was eternally perfect but not complete because He was still short of the human nature. Christ passed through the process of incarnation to possess the human nature (John 1:14).

The four Gospels have many stories about Jesus in them, and when I was young, my mother used to tell me these stories. But very few New Testament readers realize that the four Gospels are not merely composed of stories about Jesus, but are books that show us the completion of Christ. The Gospels show us a particular Person living on this earth and passing through human living. In order for Jesus to be God's anointed One, the Christ, He needed to have a human living (Phil. 2:7-8). If He had never passed through human living, how could He be our Shepherd, our High Priest, or our Helper, our Comforter? Because Christ needed to be completed in this matter, He became a man and passed through human living. Luke 2:40 and 52 tell us how the little child Jesus grew and advanced in wisdom and stature. His divine wisdom matched His growth in physical stature. He was a human boy, growing among human beings. He passed through this growth for thirty-three and a half years. This process of human living was necessary for Him to pass through so that He could be God's Christ to carry out God's eternal commission to fulfill God's divine economy.

After passing through the process of human living, Christ went through the process of crucifixion (Acts 2:23). In order for Him to be God's Anointed to carry out God's eternal commission, He needed such a death. His death annulled all the negative things and solved all the problems in the universe. After His death, He entered into resurrection (Acts 2:24). Christ was not only life but also resurrection (John 11:25). However, it was not until the day of His resurrection that He passed through resurrection and entered into resurrection in His physical experience. He was Jesus in the form of the physical flesh for thirty-three and a half years, but He needed to be in the form of the Spirit. He needed to be not only the physical Christ, but also the pneumatic Christ. He passed through resurrection and came out of that resurrection to be in another form, in the form of the life-giving Spirit (1 Cor. 15:45). That He could be such a Christ with a body of flesh yet resurrected in the divine life is a wonderful mystery (John 20:19-20). Thank the Lord that in the entire universe there is such a resurrection.

To fulfill God's eternal purpose, Christ needed to be divinely equipped with these four items: incarnation, human living, the all-inclusive crucifixion, and the wonderful resurrection. Now we have a Christ with this great and divine equipment. In His resurrection He became a life-giving Spirit. We have to see the four Gospels in the light of the completion of Christ. The four Gospels do not merely tell us stories of Jesus performing miraculous things. We have to see that the greatest miracles are the incarnation, human living, death, and resurrection of the wonderful Jesus. Today Jesus is different than He was before His incarnation. Through His incarnation, He partook of blood and flesh (Heb. 2:14) to become a man. Through His crucifixion and in His resurrection He was transfigured from the flesh into a life-giving Spirit.

On the evening of the day of resurrection, the Lord came with a resurrected body (Luke 24:37-40; 1 Cor. 15:44) into the room where the disciples were with the doors shut. We may say that He could do this because He was a Spirit, yet He showed His disciples His hands and His side (John 20:20). After eight days, the Lord appeared to His disciples again in the room where the doors were shut. He asked Thomas to touch His hands and His side so that he would believe (20:27). Our limited mentality cannot comprehend this, but it is a fact. If someone asks you whether Jesus was a physical person when He appeared to the disciples in resurrection, the best response is, "I don't know." This Jesus is a person whom we can never know with our limited mentality. In His resurrected body it is hard to say whether Christ is physical or spiritual, but we do know that in the universe there is such a marvelous thing as the resurrection of Jesus.

Now Christ is fully equipped with incarnation, human living, crucifixion, and resurrection. In resurrection He became a life-giving Spirit, the essential Spirit of life (1 Cor. 15:45; John 20:22). His becoming such a Spirit through His death and resurrection cut a new and living way for Him to impart life into us and for us to receive Him as this very life. Without such a new and living way cut by His death and resurrection, there would be no way for God to impart His divine life into any sinners and no way for any sinner to receive God as his life. The new and living way is the way cut by Jesus' death and resurrection. Now He is the life-giving Spirit, the very pneumatic Christ, the essential Spirit of life.

The next step in the completion of Christ was His ascension (Acts 2:33-36). He entered not only into resurrection but also into ascension. We have a Christ in ascension, and we are in a Christ who is in ascension. He is in ascension, and since we are in Him, we are also in ascension (Eph. 2:6). Whenever I speak, I have the realization that I am speaking from ascension and in ascension. In resurrection Christ became a life-giving Spirit, the essential Spirit of life, and in ascension He became a powerful Christ, the economical Spirit of power (Acts 2:1-4, 33b). In resurrection He is the life-giving Spirit in the essence of the divine Being. But if He had never entered into ascension, He would not have received the authority. As a man, He would have never been enthroned (Heb. 12:2b) and crowned with glory and honor (Heb. 2:9). Today, Christ is a person in ascension who has been glorified, enthroned, and entrusted with all the authority in heaven and on earth (Matt. 28:18).

LINKED TO THE COMPLETED CHRIST

The first major item in the divine economy is the completion of Christ. When God created the present universe, He spent only six days. But for God to complete Christ, He spent thirty-three and a half years. God went through a long process to finish the completion of His Christ. Today our Savior is such a completed Christ. He has been completed in incarnation, in human living, in crucifixion, in resurrection, in becoming the essential Spirit of life, in ascension, and in becoming the economical Spirit of power. When we go out to knock on doors we are persons linked to this One. This Christ has linked us to Himself, and by this linking He sends us to people as His ambassadors. When the heretical Mormons and Jehovah's Witnesses go to knock on people's doors, they are not linked to this Christ. There is no incarnation, human living, all-inclusive death, wonderful resurrection, essential Spirit of life, ascension, or economical Spirit of power in their knocking. But when we go out, we go out with all the equipment of the completed Christ.

I was told that when some young saints first went out to visit people by knocking on their doors, they were shaking with fear. If you go out to visit people by knocking on their doors and you shake, that means you have never received the vision that you are linked to the completed Christ. If a vision is imparted into us through the fellowship in this message, our hand and our arm will not shake when we knock on the door, but will be stronger than steel. The hand with which you knock on people's doors is not a common hand but a hand with incarnation, human living, the all-inclusive death, the wonderful resurrection, the becoming of the essential Spirit, the ascension, and the becoming of the economical Spirit. Our knocking on people's doors is a great thing.

Some told me that they were amazed when they went out to knock on doors and the people whom they visited were baptized within a short time. Although this may be surprising to us, it is not surprising to the Lord. He told us that all authority had been given to Him in heaven and on earth, and He charged us to go with this universal authority (Matt. 28:18-19). This universal authority is composed of and with Christ's deity, Christ's incarnation, Christ's human living, Christ's death, Christ's resurrection, Christ's being the life-giving Spirit, Christ's ascension, and Christ's being the economical Spirit of power. We are going out with this authority composed of all these items.

This authority makes you a great person. If the

President of the United States were to come to your home, his prestige would become his authority and his power to subdue you to the uttermost. You would be subdued by his presidency. In like manner, you have to realize that when you go out to knock on people's doors, you are the greatest person on this earth. You are a person who is linked to the completed Christ with all the authority in heaven and on earth entrusted to you. To knock on people's doors, preach the gospel to them, and lead them to be baptized is the way of authority, the God-ordained way to spread the gospel.

I received some negative reports from some, telling me that knocking on doors does not work. One person told me that he went out for twenty days without one being baptized. This is like Peter going fishing for the whole night, and not catching one fish (John 21:3). For Peter to fish all night at the right time for fishing and catch nothing was amazing. If he had caught one hundred fish, that would not have been amazing but normal. For us Christians, the ambassadors of Christ, to go out and knock on people's doors for twenty days without one being baptized is amazing. When I was in Taipei, some were ecstatic when they told me that they baptized five in one evening. Such an occurrence, however, should be normal to us because we are great persons who are linked to the completed Christ, the processed Christ. To visit people by knocking on their doors and getting many baptized may be a wonder to us. To the Lord, however, it is not. To Him it is normal.

Who is going to visit people by knocking on their doors so that millions can get baptized? We have to be the ones to bear this responsibility, but we need to ask ourselves what kind of persons we are. Are we linked to such a completed Christ or are we linked to ourselves? We need to go out as persons linked with this completed Christ.

Without completing this Christ, God could do nothing. We can see how God's anointed One was being completed in the four Gospels in incarnation, human living, death, and resurrection. At the end of the four Gospels He came back with all these qualifications as the life-giving Spirit to breathe Himself into His disciples, who received Him as life. Then this Christ entered into ascension so that He could clothe the believers with Himself as the economical Spirit of power. God needed to complete Christ so that He could carry out His eternal purpose through this Christ, in this Christ, and with this Christ. Christ has gone through such a marvelous process, and today we are in the processed Christ, the completed Christ. I have the burden to pass this vision on to every Christian.

Some have said that knocking on people's doors may work in Taiwan, but not work in other countries and areas of the world. I do not agree with this. Our success depends upon whether or not we have been linked to this completed Christ. If we are linked to this completed Christ, we can break through any barrier. All the authority in heaven and on earth has been given to this Christ, and He commissioned us to go to disciple the nations. The completed Christ of God is in us and with us. By being linked to this wonderful One, we can fulfill His commission.

THE PROPAGATION OF THE PNEUMATIC CHRIST

The next major item in the divine economy is the propagation of the pneumatic Christ. In the book of Acts, the completed Christ was being propagated, multiplied; on the day of Pentecost three thousand were baptized (Acts 2:41). To knock on people's doors and to preach the gospel to them is to make them the multiplication of the pneumatic Christ. The gospel will make sinners a multiplication of the pneumatic, completed Christ.

This pneumatic Christ is the essential Spirit of life to impart the divine life of resurrection into God's chosen and believing people (John 3:3, 5-6). We are not able to impart Christ to everyone. We will be able to impart Christ only to those who were chosen by God. In Luke 10 the Lord told the disciples that He was sending them as lambs in the midst of wolves (v. 3). However, among these wolves there are a good number of sons of peace who are God's chosen people (v. 6). Our trainees in Taipei have the experience of being able to discern whether or not a person is a son of peace within a few minutes. A person may not be a son of peace on your first visit to him. But after a second or third visit, he may become a son of peace.

The pneumatic Christ is also the economical Spirit of power to baptize the regenerated believers into one Body (1 Cor. 12:13). When we preach the gospel to the people whom we are visiting and they open up themselves to the Lord by praying to Him and calling upon His name, two things immediately occur: they get regenerated, and they get baptized into one Body with millions of believers. We need such a clear vision to see what a great thing it is to go out by being linked to Christ so that people can be regenerated with the essential, pneumatic Christ and baptized not only into the Triune God but also into the Body of Christ. These two things occur immediately when a new one calls on the name of the Lord. At that time, these new ones may not be able to apprehend this much, but gradually as they grow in life, they will enter into the real vision of these wonderful truths.

We have seen some newly baptized ones enter into the full realization of these truths within half a year. In Taipei, we first set up meetings in people's homes, and then we combined three or four homes together as a group. Finally, we combined a number of groups together for a community meeting. These communities set up their own hall by renting a place. They set up their own meeting and an offering box. These new ones in the communities are the elders, the deacons, and the attendants who do all the functioning. I would like to see this repeated in all the cities in the United States. We do not want to see anything of degraded Christianity.

THE PRODUCING OF THE CHURCH

Through our going out to knock on people's doors, we bring them God's completed Christ as the very pneumatic One, who is the essential Spirit of life and the economical Spirit of power, to produce regenerated and baptized believers. The church is produced organically by imparting God's completed Christ into sinners to make them regenerated and baptized members of one Body. This one Body is the church, which is produced with the unsearchable riches of the processed Christ (Eph. 3:8). The unsearchable riches of this processed Christ are divine, heavenly, spiritual, and mysterious, yet they are so real and practical. By enjoying the unsearchable riches of this processed Christ, we all become members of His Body, which is the church. The Body of Christ is the fullness of Christ, the expression of Christ (Eph. 3:6), and the organism of the Triune God (John 15:1-5).

When we enjoy the riches of Christ, we become the fullness of Christ. This means that when we experience Christ, we will become His very expression. The husky, young American men, who assimilate so much of the rich American food, are the fullness of America. They are the expression of the riches of America, and this expression is the fullness produced by the riches. Christ possesses unsearchable riches. If we enjoy these riches, we will become His very expression, His fullness. The church today must be the fullness of the One who fills all in all. This is according to God's eternal plan (Eph. 3:11) to accomplish the mystery hidden in God from the ages (v. 9). We need to practice the new way as persons who are linked with Christ and who go out with Christ to impart this Christ to people as life and as power that they might be regenerated and baptized for the producing of the church.

CHAPTER TWO

THE DIVINE TRINITY'S OPERATION

Scripture Reading: 1 Cor. 12:1-12

THE SUBJECT OF FIRST CORINTHIANS

First Corinthians 12:1-12 is a portion of the Word that has been misunderstood and even misused throughout the history of the church. To understand any section or any sentence of the holy Word, one needs a complete and overall view of the entire Bible. The twelve verses in the Scripture reading are one short section of 1 Corinthians, and to understand them we need to see what 1 Corinthians talks about.

In the last century the Brethren taught that 1 Corinthians was a book to solve the problems in the church life. The first of the eleven problems in 1 Corinthians is the problem of division (1:10-17). They considered the portion from chapter twelve through chapter fourteen as a section on the problem of the gifts. In particular, the Brethren felt that this section of 1 Corinthians was written to solve the problem of tongue-speaking. Apparently Paul wrote this letter to solve all the problems, but actually there was a deeper thought and burden within Paul. Those in Pentecostalism stress very much that 1 Corinthians is the unique book in the New Testament and in the entire Bible that encourages us to speak in tongues. Actually, however, in 1 Corinthians Paul strongly belittles the gift of tongues and exalts the gift of prophecy, because his main concern is the church, not the individual believers. Speaking in tongues, even if it is genuine and proper, edifies only the speaker himself, but prophesying, to speak forth the Lord, builds up the church (14:1-4).

The position of 1 Corinthians in the Bible bears a particular significance. The arrangement of the books of the Bible was under God's sovereignty. Malachi could not be the first book of the Old Testament nor could Genesis be the last book. Psalms and Proverbs are properly placed before the prophets and not after. In the New Testament it is significant that Matthew comes first and that Revelation is last. The four Gospels give us a clear view of the completion of Christ. God anointed His Son to be His Christ, yet even His Son, the God-anointed One, needed to be completed, to be equipped, in order that He might have the ability and the qualifications to carry out His commission to accomplish God's eternal plan. Thus, the four Gospels tell us how God's Son has been completed to be God's Christ to carry out God's New Testament economy. Acts tells us how this completed Christ was propagated. Due to this propagation, many believers came into existence. Thus, we need Romans to tell us what the Christian life is for the church life. Romans shows us the Christian life for the church life, and 1 Corinthians follows to show us how to have the church life.

The practice of today's Christianity is a destruction of the church life. Unrestricted speaking in tongues is a great destruction to the proper church life, and it destroyed the church life at Corinth. In 1 Corinthians 12—14 Paul dealt with tongue-speaking to save the saints in Corinth from the destruction of the church life. He adjusted the Corinthian believers in many ways that they might have a proper church life. The proper church life depends absolutely upon the church meetings. If we do not have proper church meetings, we can never have a proper church life. The term "church" is *ekklesia* in Greek, which means the called out assembly. This term implies meeting because the church is an assembly. Without the meetings, there is no church. How to have the meetings, however, is a big problem to the church life. Today on this entire earth it is hard to find the proper church life because there are not the proper church meetings.

THE LORD'S NEW WAY

The Lord's new way is mainly to bring people into the church and then to form them into meetings that they may enter into the proper church life for the building up of Christ's universal Body. The visiting of people's homes by knocking on their doors is the God-ordained way to spread the gospel. To have meetings set up in the new believers' homes is also God's ordained way to begin the church life. After God has done so much to complete Christ and to propagate Christ to produce the church life, we have to see how the church should meet, and the way for the church to meet is by the divine Trinity's operation. In every church meeting is the divine Trinity's operation. The Christian gathering is for the divine Trinity to operate for the purpose of carrying out the dispensing of the processed Triune God. The way to continue God's New Testament economy is to have meetings for the Triune God to operate among us to carry out His dispensing of the processed Trinity. Christianity has lost the view of God's New Testament economy and has lost the view of God's ordained way to carry out this economy.

The Lord's new way is not merely the way to knock on doors or the way to set up meetings in people's homes. The Lord's new way is to carry out God's New Testament economy. God's New Testament economy is first to complete His Christ and then to propagate, to duplicate, to reproduce, this completed Christ and dispense Him into His chosen and believing people for the producing of the church, which is the organism of the Triune God. This divine organism exists, is maintained, and goes on by being gathered into the Lord's name (Matt. 18:20), the highest name in the universe. In such a gathering, the Triune God operates. God the Father operates, the Son ministers, and the Spirit distributes all the gifts for the dispensing of the processed Triune God (1 Cor. 12:4-6).

The purpose for us Christians to meet is unique. It is not for teaching, for preaching, for tongue-speaking, for healing, or for miracles. The Christian meeting is for the dispensing of the processed Triune God. Many Bible teachers do not realize that the teaching of the Bible should be for the Triune God to operate so that He can carry out the dispensing of His divine Triune self. Even the gospel preaching is not for gospel preaching but for the Triune God to operate to carry out His divine dispensing of Himself. We are not merely going to recover door knocking or home meetings. We believe the Lord has shown us a way to recover the divine dispensing of the divine Being into our being. The Lord's new way for His new move is to recover the proper way of gospel preaching and the proper way of Christian meeting that the Triune God may operate among His chosen people to dispense Himself into their being.

After the completion of God's Christ, the propagation of the pneumatic Christ, and the producing of the church, the divine Trinity is looking for and expecting to have a proper opportunity among His chosen people so that He can operate among them and within them to dispense Himself into them. Our past way to meet did not afford God much of an opportunity to dispense Himself into us. In most Christian meetings today God has nearly no way to operate in order to dispense Himself into His chosen people. God needs to recover this way that He may have on this earth in many places around the globe groups of seeking Christians who afford Him the opportunity to operate in them so He can dispense Himself into their being.

In every Christian meeting, God should be operating, and this operation is carried out by ministries, which are completed by the different gifts of the Holy Spirit. In 1 Corinthians 12:4-6 there is a picture of the Triune God that begins with the Spirit, goes through the Lord, and reaches God the Father. With the Spirit is the distribution of the gifts, with the Lord are the ministries, and with God the Father are the operations. God the Father operates, the Lord ministers through different ministries, and the Spirit distributes Himself into the believers as gifts. Thus, all the gifts are accomplishing the ministries, and all the ministries are carrying out God's operation. The operation of the divine Trinity is to carry out the divine dispensing of the divine Being into us, the believers in Christ, that we may become His organism to express Him in the whole earth. This is the new way for the Lord's new move.

THE SPIRIT MOVING THE BELIEVERS
TO SAY "LORD JESUS"
AND DISTRIBUTING GIFTS TO THE BELIEVERS

In the divine Trinity's operation, the Spirit moves the believers to say "Lord Jesus" and distributes gifts to the believers (1 Cor. 12:3-4). In many Christian meetings on this earth, the attendants come in an orderly and quiet way to be seated. They sit there waiting for a pastor to stand up to say something to them. This is the killing way to meet. These believers may have been very living, active, and talkative outside the chapel. But when they came into that chapel, their function and their livingness was killed. Even in the local churches we somewhat practice this way. We may have been quite active outside the meeting hall, but when we came into the meeting hall, we sat down and waited for one of the elders to say something. We need to come into the meeting hall calling, "O Lord Jesus!" What a meeting that would be if all of us would function to begin the meeting by calling upon the name of the Lord. In many Christian meetings certain people sing solos. Everyone in the audience keeps quiet to listen to that solo, and their function is killed. Then there may be a quartet, and after their singing the issue is death. We need to reject this dead way of meeting.

When we call "O Lord Jesus," this will stir all of us up, revive us, and make us alive. The more you say "O Lord Jesus," the more you will be alive, and the more you will enliven others. When we call "O Lord Jesus," we not only sense the very presence of the living Christ, but we also have the sensation that Someone is moving and living within us. Some might say that if we all called on the Lord in the meeting that this would make too much noise. But God likes to have noise; He does not like our quietness in the meetings. The Psalms tell us to make a joyful noise unto the Lord (66:1; 81:1; 95:1-2; 98:4, 6; 100:1). The Psalms do not say that we need to have a joyful voice. A voice is something that is in order, but a noise is made when everyone is speaking.

You may feel that others can speak and function but

that you have no gift to speak and function. Actually, however, you are not poor. Your poverty comes through your dumbness. Romans 10:12 tells us that the Lord is rich to all who call upon Him. After ten times of calling "O Lord Jesus," you will have something to say. Calling on the name of the Lord stirs you up from within. When you call upon the Lord, you have the gift, and you want to flow out to others.

The first three verses of 1 Corinthians 12 give us a new start for our meetings. When we come to the meeting and we are all dumb, we will lose our function. We will not know what to say. But after a few times of calling "O Lord Jesus," we will have a burden to say something. Try calling on the name of the Lord Jesus in a meeting ten times, and see what will come out. After ten times of calling on the Lord's name, we would not be able to sit down, and we would have to flow out from within. At the same time that we call on the Lord's name, the Spirit distributes the gift into us. If we want to function in the meeting, the way to get the gift is by calling on the name of the Lord. Everyone among us should try this.

In 1933 I began to work together with Brother Nee. He always stressed that in the meetings one or two brothers should not be the only ones who speak. He stressed that everybody should learn to speak. At that time I wondered how we could help the saints function in the meetings. After many years of study, I began to see the first three verses of 1 Corinthians 12: "Now concerning spiritual gifts, brothers, I do not want you to be ignorant. You know that when you were of the nations, you were led away to dumb idols, however you were led. Wherefore I make known to you that no one speaking in the Spirit of God says, Jesus is accursed; and no one can say, Lord Jesus, except in the Holy Spirit." From these verses, how do we know that we are speaking in the Spirit of God? It is by calling on the Lord's name. When we call, that is a sign that the Spirit of God is moving in us. No one can say, "Lord Jesus," except in the Holy Spirit. To say "Lord Jesus" is the start of the Spirit's distribution of the gifts in verse 4, which says, "But there are distributions of gifts, but the same Spirit." The beginning of the distribution of the gifts by the Spirit is our calling "Lord Jesus." The best way to help the saints to function or to speak in the meetings is to charge them, to motivate them, to call on the name of the Lord Jesus.

In the early seventies when we were meeting in Elden Hall in Los Angeles, our meetings were always in the heavenlies because there was so much calling on the name of the Lord. The saints were calling on the name of the Lord in their homes and on their way to the meeting hall. Thus, whenever you entered into the meeting place, you had the sensation that you were alive and that everything was living there. All of this calling on the name of the Lord ushered in the speaking from all the saints. We did not have enough time in our meetings for everybody to speak. Gradually, however, our calling on the name of the Lord has diminished, has slowed down. Thus, our meetings also began to be very slow.

Now the rescue is to call on name of the Lord. This calling stirs up the distribution of the gifts. Then the gifts perform all kinds of ministries by the Lord, and all these ministries will carry out the operation of the Father. This operation through the ministries by the gifts will dispense the divine Trinity into our being. In our meetings there should be no formalities nor rituals. We need to come in calling on the name of the Lord and begin to speak. To keep the formalities and rituals is to remain in death.

THE GATHERING OF GOD'S PEOPLE IN THE OLD DISPENSATION

The gathering of God's people in the old dispensation was with Christ prefigured in all the types, but not completed through all the processes. Today we have the real Christ completed through all the processes. The gathering of God's people in the old dispensation was also with regulations of letters only and no direction and move by the Spirit. Today in the Christian meetings there must not be the regulations of letters but the direction and move by the Spirit. Finally, in the old dispensation, the gathering of God's people had patterns only of things to come and no accomplishments for God's eternal plan. Today it should be that in every meeting God operates to accomplish something according to His plan.

CHAPTER THREE

THE DEFORMED AND DEGRADED CHRISTIANITY

Scripture Reading: Rev. 2:14-15, 20; 3:1-2

In the past two chapters we have seen the positive items of the divine economy and of the divine Trinity's operation. In this chapter we want to see an item that is altogether negative. We need to compare what is seen in the Bible with what is seen today in Christianity. I have to use two words to describe today's Christianity: deformed and degraded. If we are not careful, we might become something that is deformed and degraded. All of Christianity is deformed from the form of the revelation in the holy Word and is also degraded. We need to know the real situation and see a clear picture of today's Christianity. When we talk about Christianity in such a way, this does not mean that we do not love all Christians. We love all of our brothers and sisters in the Lord, yet we have to admit that today's Christendom is absolutely far off from God's eternal plan.

THE PICTURE OF TODAY'S CHRISTENDOM IN MATTHEW 13

This deformed and degraded religious system is fully covered by the Lord in a prophetic way in three parables in Matthew 13. The first four parables of this chapter form one group, and the last three form another group. Three of these first four parables give us a picture of today's Christendom. One parable shows us that while the wheat is growing the enemy of the Lord comes and sows tares amidst the wheat (vv. 24-30). This means that the false believers, the nominal Christians, were sown into the so-called church. In degraded Christianity there are many false or nominal Christians. Only about twenty percent of the members of the denomination in which my mother was a member were genuine Christians. Even though my mother attended that denomination and loved Christianity, she was not saved until the Lord used me to raise up a local church in our town.

In today's Christianity there are also modernists, who do not recognize the inspiration of the holy Word and deny the Lord's incarnation through the virgin Mary. They say that the Lord's death was not for redemption but only a kind of martyrdom. They believe that the Lord was martyred on the cross for His teachings which were different from the Jewish traditional religion. They also deny the resurrection of Christ and all the miracles in the Bible. This modernistic teaching spread even to China, and fifty years ago it was prevailing on the college campuses. We had to fight against this teaching in mainland China, and eventually the Lord gained the victory. Today there are hardly any modernists among the Christians on the mainland of China. Second Peter 2:1 says that such modernists are degraded to such an extent that they even deny the Master who bought them. The false teachers at Peter's time, like today's modernists in their apostasy, denied both the Lord's person as the Master and His redemption, by which the Lord purchased the believers.

Another parable in Matthew 13 describes today's Christendom as a great tree with great branches that become a lodging place for birds (vv. 31-32). This is the parable of the mustard seed. The mustard is an annual herb, which shows that the church should be like an herb to produce food. Instead it became a tree, a lodge for birds, having its nature and function changed. These birds refer to Satan's evil spirits with the evil persons and things motivated by them (13:4, 19). They lodge in the branches of the great tree, that is, in the enterprises of Christendom. Today's Catholic Church is full of all kinds of evils. Evil persons, evil practices, and evil things are lodging there. In this great organization there is much darkness.

Another parable describing the situation of Christendom

THE DEFORMED AND DEGRADED CHRISTIANITY 27

is the parable of the woman who took the leaven and put it into the fine flour (13:33-35). This woman, prophesied by the Lord in Matthew 13:33, is mentioned in Revelation 2:20. She was typified by Jezebel in the Old Testament and fulfilled by the Roman Catholic Church. The Roman Catholic Church became such an adulterous woman who added leaven (signifying evil, heretical, and pagan things) into the fine flour (signifying Christ as the meal offering for the satisfaction of God and man). The Catholic Church took in all kinds of pagan practices. G. H. Pember pointed out that Catholicism even took in Buddha under the name of Saint Josaphat. The story of this saint named Josaphat is actually that of Buddha.

Roman Catholicism is depicted in Revelation 17 as a great prostitute and as "The Mother of the Prostitutes" (vv. 1, 5). Since The Mother of the Prostitutes is the apostate church, the prostitutes, her daughters, should be all the different sects and groups in Christianity who hold to some extent the teaching, practices, and traditions of the apostate Roman Church. *The Two Babylons* is a book that gives a full documentation of the deformation and degradation of this evil religious system. G. H. Pember in his book, *The Great Prophecies*, also points out the abominations of the apostate Roman Catholic Church. The Brethren also saw the real situation of Catholicism, and we received much help from them. The entire Christianity is the totality of deformation and degradation.

In the 1920s on mainland China a number of us young people left this deformed religion. We thank the Lord for sending the western missionaries to China to bring us the gospel. They told people that Jesus is the Son of God who became a man and died on the cross for our sins. They said that if we believe in Him we would receive the forgiveness of our sins. We heard the proper preaching of Christ being our Savior. These missionaries also brought us the real name of Jesus Christ, and we treasured this. They also brought the Bible with them, providing us with one of the best Chinese translations of the Bible. We thank God for these three things: the gospel, the name of Jesus, and the

Bible. We young people who came out of Christendom made a decision just to keep these three things. We would not have anything to do with the remaining unscriptural things in Christianity. We came out of this deformed system, and the Lord led us to begin the church life for the first time in Brother Nee's hometown. From that time we have been suffering persecution, not mainly from the unbelievers, but from Christianity.

We love all our Christian brothers and respect them, yet we cannot agree with the religious system they are in. There are many genuine believers even in the Catholic Church, and some of them are seeking and devout. Yet the Catholic Church itself is full of idolatry. In some cathedrals the ones who enter buy a candle and select an idol to pray to. They do not call these statues idols but saints. A certain Catholic cathedral in Manila has a statue of a "black Jesus," and all the people who go into this cathedral touch the feet of that statue. I watched the people buy candles and go in to worship the idols, and I read some of the inscriptions on the wall, which said that if you pray to a certain saint for a period of time, your relatives would be rescued from purgatory. This shows that Catholicism is full of superstition. This fellowship should give us a glimpse of the practice in today's degraded Christianity.

LEAVING THE GOD-ORDAINED WAY FOR CARRYING OUT THE NEW TESTAMENT ECONOMY

The deformed and degraded Christianity has left the God-ordained way for carrying out the New Testament economy. Christianity does not care for the New Testament economy, but God does. God's New Testament economy is first to complete His Christ and then to propagate this completed, pneumatic Christ to produce the church. The entire Christianity is far away from this economy, having left the God-ordained way to carry out God's eternal purpose.

TAKING THE NATURAL, HUMAN, TRADITIONAL, CULTURAL, AND RELIGIOUS WAY

This degraded religious system takes the natural,

THE DEFORMED AND DEGRADED CHRISTIANITY 29

human, traditional, cultural, and religious way. Humanly speaking, religion is a good thing, but spiritually speaking it is something against God's economy. God does not want a religion, but He surely wants to see His economy accomplished. We are not here for religion but for God's economy, which is to propagate His completed Christ to produce the church as the Body of such a Christ. Christianity is not focused on the divine economy but is a human religion saturated with demonic and satanic things. This natural, human, traditional, and cultural religion is full of organizations. Without organizations, Christianity could not survive. The Catholic Church and all the denominations depend upon organization. Although we do not like to have organization, sometimes the leading brothers in some of the localities brought in and trusted in their organization. We must realize that organization kills. We trust in the living Spirit. The church as the Body of Christ should be a divine organism full of the living Spirit.

Christianity is also full of formalities and rituals. The new way that we are taking to carry out God's New Testament economy has nothing to do with formalities and rituals. In Taipei we practiced to baptize the new ones immediately after they received the Lord. Sometimes the husband got baptized one day, and the next day he baptized his wife. A father was baptized one week, and the next week he baptized his son. The New Testament shows us that whoever preaches the gospel has the right to baptize those that they bring to the Lord.

In the past, we would not baptize someone unless he passed through the examination of the elders. As a result, a person who received the Lord could not be baptized immediately, but he had to wait. Sometimes a candidate for baptism could not pass the examination of the elders so he was encouraged to learn more and come back next month to see if he could be baptized then. This practice is a formality that is not according to the Scriptures. In the book of Acts, whenever someone believed in the Lord, he was immediately baptized (8:35-38; 16:14-15, 31-33; cf. Mark

16:16). There was no waiting to be baptized. To wait is wrong. Mark 16:16 tells us to believe and be baptized. This is one complete step for salvation. Many in Christianity teach that we need to believe in the Lord Jesus and receive Him, but they will not baptize a person unless that person has passed through a formal examination. We should not practice any kind of formality.

The deformed and degraded Christianity is also full of regulations and of unscriptural practices. The celebration of Christmas is an example of an unscriptural and even pagan practice. Centuries before the Christian era, on December 25 the European pagans celebrated the birthday of the sun. When Constantine embraced Christianity, he encouraged the Roman citizens to become Christians, and he even rewarded many thousands for being baptized. Thousands who knew nothing of Christ were baptized and came into Christendom, bringing their pagan customs with them. Later, the name of Christ was attached to the birth of the sun god celebrated on December 25. We should have nothing to do with such unscriptural and even pagan practices.

KILLING THE LIVING MEMBERS
OF THE BODY OF CHRIST

The religious system of today's Christendom also kills the living members of the Body of Christ. To some extent Christianity brings many people to the name of Christ in a good way. However, after people enter into Christianity, their function is bound and eventually killed. Nearly every so-called church service kills the function of the people there. Thus, the very people who have been brought to the Lord in Christianity are killed in their function. In the new way we need to stand against killing the living members of the Body of Christ. On the other hand, we need to be those who make people alive.

ANNULLING THE ORGANIC FUNCTION
OF THE MEMBERS OF CHRIST

Furthermore, the deformed and degraded Christianity

THE DEFORMED AND DEGRADED CHRISTIANITY 31

annuls the organic function of the members of Christ. About thirty years ago in Manila a group of brothers among us went to visit a sick person in the hospital. The brothers who went to visit this sick person all prayed one by one, and his relatives, who were also Christians, were shocked. They asked whether or not these brothers were pastors. They were told that none of them was a pastor but that all of them were just brothers. The relatives of this sick person said that they did not know how to pray and that they never prayed. They thought that praying was the job of a pastor. The prevailing concept in today's Christianity is that preaching, teaching the Bible, and praying for others is the pastor's job. A person goes to a pastor in the same way that he would go to an attorney or a doctor for specific services. This clergy-laity system annuls the functions of the members of Christ. The attendants in the so-called Christian services go there and do nothing. They do not know how to do anything. They only know how to sit there and watch a few others function. In the church life there should not be an annulling of others' functions but a stirring up of everyone to function.

In the community meetings of the new believers in Taipei, they were all encouraged to function. In the training in Taipei, we charged the trainees not to replace the new ones in their home meetings. They are charged not to act as a pastor. They must behave like an ordinary, little brother among all the new converts, and they have to give place to everyone. They should not replace anyone. This is why the result of the Lord's move in Taipei has been so successful. The new believers in these communities are encouraged to function to the uttermost. They have their own home meetings and they themselves either rent a place or have a place in a home where the whole community can come together. They even set up their own offering box. They do everything by themselves, and they are not told what to do. We recently had a burden to purchase some land in Taipei. When these new believers heard this, they began to give for the purchase of this land.

We must believe that every believer is a living one because every believer has the living God, Christ, the Spirit of life, in him. We should afford every believer an opportunity to express his living situation as a living member of the Body of Christ. In today's Christianity the living members are killed, and their functions are annulled.

OPENING THE WAY FOR THE NOMINAL CHRISTIANS TO MOVE AND ACT IN THE SO-CALLED CHURCHES

Christianity also opens the way for the nominal Christians to move and act in the so-called churches. We have already mentioned this point in our fellowship concerning the tares. The tares are false believers, believers only in name, who do not have the divine life in them. The Lord tells us that the tares are the sons of the evil one (Matt. 13:38). The judgment upon the tares will be so serious (vv. 40-42) because they have been confusing, frustrating, and damaging God's economy. In the eyes of God, the tares are exceedingly evil. Christianity is full of false believers.

BUILDING UP HIERARCHY

Christendom also builds up hierarchy. The hierarchy in the Catholic Church has been fully established with the pope as the head followed by the cardinals, the archbishops, and the bishops. The woman depicted in Revelation 17 is clothed in scarlet (v. 4). The color scarlet is found everywhere in the Vatican. The most striking use of scarlet is in the garb of the cardinals, who have red hats and red robes. The daughters of the great prostitute in Revelation 17 follow their mother in this matter of hierarchy. Which denomination has no hierarchy? The highest degree of hierarchy can be found in The Mother of the Prostitutes while a lower degree of hierarchy is practiced and found with her daughters. Therefore, we must hate any kind of hierarchy.

If the elders in the local churches consider themselves higher than others, that is the satanic thought of hierarchy. There is no hierarchy among us. No one in the churches is higher than others. Everybody is the same. The thought of hierarchy is in our fallen nature. Everyone likes to be a king or a leader. Some brothers are ambitious to be elders, and some wives of elders feel that they are above others. The wives of the elders should not consider themselves as queens but as wives of slaves. All the elders are slaves to the saints. It is a shame for an elder's wife to consider her husband higher than others. The Lord Jesus Himself exposed this matter of ambition and hierarchy in Matthew 20:20-28 and 23:1-12. For me to consider myself higher than another brother is shameful. If you consider me to be higher than you, the satanic thought of hierarchy is in your mind. We all have to love each other and respect one another, yet we should not consider anyone to be higher than others. Among us there is only One who is higher than everybody—the Lord Jesus. All of Christendom is filled with hierarchy.

UTILIZING THE BIG MEETING AS A FACADE TO ATTRACT PEOPLE

Christendom also utilizes the big meetings as a facade to attract people into the religion of Christianity. Since October of 1984, I began to promote the small home meetings. Some of the saints thought these small home meetings were very poor in comparison to the big meetings. I attended a small home meeting in Taipei. At first I was disappointed. By the scheduled time of meeting there were only an old man, a small girl, and a young school teacher. Gradually, however, many new ones came. The stronger saints had gone out to bring these new ones to the meeting. By the end of the meeting I was very encouraged with the functioning. Some, however, like to have the facade of the big meetings to attract people. Today's Christianity attracts people with a formal, religious gathering. When the Lord Jesus was on this earth He had a small meeting in the house in Bethany (John 12:1-3). He also ministered to a large gathering of five thousand in the wilderness (Matthew 14:14-21). This large gathering in the wilderness was full of spiritual reality, unlike the big meetings in Christianity which are full of formal attraction with little spiritual reality.

The new way for the Lord's new move in Taipei has brought in thousands of people. Since August of 1986, twenty-four thousand have been baptized and one-third of these still remain to meet in their homes. We have never had so many home meetings in our past history of thirty years in Taipei. When we had only the big meetings, we had very little increase. The attendants came to the meetings again and again to see the same faces. Whenever new ones were in the big meetings, we were happy. But very few of them remained. Eventually, many of the saints began to lose their heart for the meetings, and they only had a heart to come to see each other. Many of us have to admit that the meetings in the Lord's recovery have been lacking in power and motivation. This is why I told the church in Taipei in October of 1984 that we must drop the old way, which is a part of the degraded Christianity. We have to take care of all the saints, but not in the old way of Christianity. We have to take care of them in the new way by helping them and stirring them up to function in bringing people to the Lord and in sending meetings to people's homes. We should not merely ask the new ones to come to the church meetings, but we should bring the church meeting into their homes.

FORFEITING THE PROPER CHURCH LIFE, NOT CARING FOR THE BUILDING UP OF THE BODY OF CHRIST

Finally, the deformed and degraded Christianity forfeits the proper church life, not caring for the building up of the Body of Christ. The whole practice in today's Christianity is forfeiting and annulling the church life. There is no concern for the building up of the Body of Christ, so the divine economy is altogether dropped and missed. The Lord's new way is to recover the church life so that the Body of Christ can be built up through the church life in many localities.

My burden is to open up the real situation of today's

Christianity that we may know where we should go and where we should remain. We should stand for the testimony of Jesus in this age. We need to compare what is revealed in the Bible with what is being practiced in today's Christianity. We must stay away from the practice of the deformed and degraded Christianity and come back to the divine revelation for the Lord's recovery. The preaching of the gospel and the teaching of the Bible do take place in Christianity. But in a larger sense, the religious practice of Christianity kills the living members of Christ and annuls the organic function of the members of the Body of Christ. This religious system also involves the building up of hierarchy.

We must come back purely to the God-ordained way to practice the New Testament economy so that God can operate in His Trinity to dispense His triune being into us that we may be filled and saturated with the divine being to become His very expression on this earth. This is what God wants today. Christianity has missed this, and God is recovering this in His recovery. The way to meet is not a small matter. The traditional way of meeting kills and annuls the functions of the members of the Body of Christ and builds up something satanic and demonic. We must come back to the biblical way, the new way, the living way, that affords God the opportunity to operate among His chosen people.

CHAPTER FOUR

THE SEQUENCE OF THE DIVINE REVELATION IN THE FIRST EIGHT BOOKS OF THE NEW TESTAMENT

Scripture Reading: 1 Cor. 12:1-8; 14:3-6, 26

In this chapter we want to see the sequence of the divine revelation in the first eight books of the New Testament. The books of the Bible were written by the inspiration of God and even the arrangement of the books is also by the inspiration of the Spirit.

THE COMPLETION OF CHRIST IN MATTHEW TO JOHN

What God needed was a completed Christ, and the first thing that God did in the New Testament was to complete His Christ. Thus, the Gospels from Matthew to John unveil the completion of Christ. Many Christians know the birth of Christ, the incarnation of Christ, but they have never seen that the incarnation was the first step for God to complete His Christ. The last step of God's completion of His Christ was Christ's ascension into heaven that He might become the economical Spirit of power to be poured upon His Body. From incarnation to ascension was a process through which the Son of God, God's anointed One, was completed. Through this process He was fully equipped, fully qualified. Now He is in the heavens with all His qualifications to be God's Christ, God's anointed One, to carry out God's eternal commission.

THE PROPAGATION OF THE PNEUMATIC CHRIST IN ACTS

After the Gospels, this completed Christ was preached as the gospel. The gospel is not only a gospel of redemption, of forgiveness of sins, of life, or of grace. The gospel itself is this completed Christ. God's completed

Christ is the very essence of God's gospel. The gospel of the highest standard is God's completed Christ in God's eternal economy. This One was preached in the Acts as the gospel. Thus Acts shows us the propagation of the pneumatic Christ. Through the preaching of this completed Christ, there was a great propagation. Christ was propagated through the preaching of Himself as the gospel, so thousands of believers were produced. Three thousand were added on the day of Pentecost (Acts 2:41). Then another five thousand were added (4:4). Finally, Acts tells us that there were myriads of believers (21:20). Thousands and thousands were regenerated to be the multiplication of this completed and propagated Christ. This multiplication becomes the church. The term "the church" in Acts is not mentioned as a doctrine, a teaching, or even as a revelation, but as a practicality. The church in Jerusalem (8:1), the church in Antioch (13:1), and the churches in Syria and Cilicia (15:41) are a reality in practice. The church becomes a practicality in the book of Acts.

THE CHRISTIAN LIFE FOR
CHRIST'S BODY LIFE IN ROMANS

The regenerated ones needed to have the proper, adequate, and full knowledge of what the Christian life is and of the purpose for the Christian life. Thus, the book of Romans reveals the Christian life for Christ's Body life. The believers needed to know that the Christian life is Christ living in them and lived out of them to express Himself. The Christian life is Christ expressed for the church life. Romans tells us that we were condemned sinners (1:18—3:20) who were justified through the redemption of Christ (3:21—5:11). Then we are sanctified through the sanctifying Spirit with Christ as the sanctifying life (5:12—8:13). Romans continues to tell us that we will be glorified (8:14-39) and that we have been chosen (9:1—11:36). Chapter twelve shows us that we are members of the Body of Christ, and chapters thirteen through sixteen unveil the Christian life for the church life. Chapter sixteen of Romans shows us the local churches (vv. 1, 4-5, 16, 23). The

THE SEQUENCE OF THE DIVINE REVELATION   39

conclusion of the book of Romans is the practical church life in localities.

DEALING WITH ALL PROBLEMS FOR THE CHURCH MEETING LIFE IN FIRST CORINTHIANS

Those who are enjoying the Christian life for the church life still do not know how to meet, so the book of 1 Corinthians is needed. The book of 1 Corinthians particularly speaks concerning how to meet. First Corinthians is the only book, the unique book, that deals with all problems for the church meeting life. Chapters one through eleven and fifteen through sixteen deal with these problems by Christ as the sanctifying and transforming life (1:24, 30) through the cross of Christ (1:18, 23; 2:2). Chapters twelve through fourteen show us that these problems need to be dealt with for the church meeting life, which is by the Spirit (12:1-3), with the word (14:3-6, 26; 12:8), and through the gifts (12:4-6). Paul deals specifically with the church meetings in chapter fourteen.

The Essential, Underlying Thought of First Corinthians

We have pointed out that the Brethren say that 1 Corinthians is merely a book on how to solve all the problems in the church while those in Pentecostalism say that 1 Corinthians is the unique book that focuses on speaking in tongues. Neither of these topics, however, is the essential, underlying thought of this book. The underlying thought of 1 Corinthians is that we have to enjoy Christ. To have a proper meeting life, we do not just need to know Christ or to have a revelation concerning Him, to see Him. We have to eat Him and drink Him. Eating Jesus and drinking of Christ are the essential revelations in the book of 1 Corinthians.

In the summer of 1965 in Los Angeles we had a conference on the tree of life. In those messages the central thought was that God is good for food (see *The Tree of Life* published by Living Stream Ministry). God is edible, and

Christ is our food and our drink. The tree of life is not good for knowledge but good for food. We must break the shell of the book of 1 Corinthians to see its essential revelation. The focus of this book is not to deal with all the problems. First Corinthians shows us that we need to enjoy Christ.

The Items of Christ for Our Enjoyment in First Corinthians

There are twenty marvelous items of Christ as our enjoyment in 1 Corinthians. In chapter one Christ is our God-given portion (v. 2). God has called us into the participation of Christ, the fellowship of Christ, that is, into the enjoyment of Christ as our portion (v. 9). This is why verse 2 says that Christ is "theirs and ours." Christ is their portion and is our portion for us to enjoy. Christ is also God's power and God's wisdom to us as our righteousness concerning our past, our sanctification concerning our present, and our redemption concerning our future (1:24, 30). In chapter two Christ is the Lord of glory (v. 8) and the deep things of God (v. 10). In chapter three He is the unique foundation of God's building (v. 11). No one can lay another foundation besides Him.

In chapter five Christ is our Passover feast (v. 7). He is the Passover lamb that became a feast for us to enjoy. A feast is not good for people to know or look at but for people to eat and enjoy. In chapter five Christ is also the feast of unleavened bread as the continuation of the Passover (v. 8; cf. Exo. 12:15-20). Christ as the unleavened bread is good for eating. In chapter ten Christ is the spiritual food, the spiritual drink, and the spiritual rock, out of which flows the living water (vv. 3-4). Christ as the real rock is following His believers and flowing out the living water to satisfy their thirst. In chapter eleven Christ is the head of every man (v. 3). In chapter twelve Christ is the Body (v. 12). How marvelous that Christ is both the Head and the Body. If we are in Christ all the members of Christ become an enjoyment to us. When we are in Christ all of us are excellent, wonderful, and enjoyable people.

In chapter fifteen Christ is the firstfruit of resurrection

(vv. 20, 23). Fruit, as the issue and produce of life, is good for eating. Christ is the firstfruit for us to enjoy, and He is also the second Man (v. 47) and the last Adam (v. 45). The first man became hopeless. If there were only one man in this universe, we would not have any hope. But with the second man, Christ, there is a new beginning and there is hope. As the firstfruit, the second man, and the last Adam, Christ is everything. He is the first, the second, and the last. Christ, being the last Adam, is the conclusion of Adam. With Him and in Him Adam is over. Adam has caused us much trouble. He brought us sin, death, the curse, sufferings, and sickness. But Adam is finished, concluded, with Christ because Christ is the last Adam. Eventually Christ as the last Adam became a life-giving Spirit (15:45). If Christ were not the life-giving Spirit, all that He is would have nothing to do with us. But as the life-giving Spirit, He makes every item of Himself so real and so practical.

Calling on the Name of the Lord to Enjoy Christ as Everything for the Church Meeting Life

By calling, "O Lord Jesus," we can enjoy Him as everything, as every item in 1 Corinthians. When we say "O Lord Jesus," we enjoy Him as the foundation. "O Lord Jesus"—we enjoy Him as the first, the second, and the last. "O Lord Jesus"—we enjoy Him as food and as drink. We have to learn how to "O Lord Jesus!"

Calling "O Lord Jesus" issues in a constant, warming presence within us. When we call on the Lord, there is a divine presence within us, warming us and bringing us a bubbling joy. We need to call on the name of the Lord during every occupation, at all times, and in all places, with our mouth, in the spirit, and in the heart. We need to open our mouth, exercise our spirit, and open our heart. To call on the name of the Lord is to experience the divine Trinity.

The problems in the church life cannot be solved by any human methods. Over fifty years ago I began to labor in the ministry and often the saints came to me with problems. Most of these problems were related to marriage. I thought that I could render the saints some way to solve their problems, but eventually found out that this did not work. By reading the holy Word, I realized that we cannot solve any problem. The only way to solve people's problems is to minister this enjoyable Christ. I began to tell people that they had to experience Christ and take Christ as their life and life supply.

Although I shared these things with the saints in the 1940s I had not seen the matter of calling on the Lord's name. In the years from 1966 to 1968 we began to practice pray-reading the Word and calling on the Lord's name in Elden Hall in Los Angeles. Elden Hall is a memorial of pray-reading and calling on the name of the Lord. In one evening meeting, the saints pray-read the entire book of Ephesians. That was marvelous. Our meetings were filled with calling, "O Lord Jesus! Amen."

One day in a meeting I stood up and told the saints that all of them could say something. When I said this to the saints, I myself did not know what to tell them to say. Then I said, "All of you can say four words." At that moment I did not know what four words I would tell the saints to say. Then I said, "All of you can say O Lord, Amen, Hallelujah!" We practiced saying "O Lord, Amen, Hallelujah" for a period of time. I thought that I had made a mistake in the order of these words by telling the saints to say Amen before Hallelujah instead of saying Hallelujah, Amen. Then I checked with the New Testament. Actually, the biblical way is not "Hallelujah, Amen," but "Amen, Hallelujah" (Rev. 19:4). In those years we sang the following song again and again:

> Now Christ is the life-giving Spirit;
> Now Christ is the Spirit today.
> Now Christ is the life-giving Spirit,
> So turn to your spirit and say—
>
> O Lord, Amen!
> O Lord, Amen, Hallelujah!

THE SEQUENCE OF THE DIVINE REVELATION 43

In those days, around 1969, we were "crazy" in the enjoyment of Christ. Every day the saints would be calling, "O Lord Jesus, Amen!" Before that time we seldom said "Amen." Now to say "Amen" has become a custom among us. Today whenever you meet a brother, you say, "Amen." This brother will respond by saying "Amen" to you. Our custom of saying "Amen" came from the song mentioned above. When we say, "O Lord, Amen, Hallelujah," we have to testify that we enjoy the Lord. No one can deny this.

Some argued with me by saying that what we taught was merely a psychological thing. I responded by saying, "It may be psychological. Let us try by calling 'O George Washington!' or 'O Confucius!'" When we call on these names there is no sensation of something moving within us nor is there any feeling of enjoyment. But whenever we say "O Lord Jesus," something within is touching us, anointing us, and moving within us. The feeling within is so dear, so loving, and so sweet. In this kind of prayer there is a warming presence within us because He is living and moving within us. When we keep our mouths shut, it is hard for Him to move in us. But when we say "O Lord Jesus, Amen," He moves within us.

Sometimes people ask me, "Brother Lee, what is your secret of health? How could you live so long?" One of the secrets is "O Lord Jesus." If you have a problem with indigestion, try calling "O Lord Jesus" for five minutes. Calling will help you to digest your food. Calling on the Lord will make you happy, will take away your burdens, and will especially take away your human anxiety. In human life day by day there is continuous anxiety. Those who call "O Lord Jesus" again and again throughout the day do not have anxiety. By calling on the Lord all our anxiety will be gone. The Lord is living within us. We need to open our mouth, exercise our spirit, and open our heart to release Jesus by calling on His name. In this way we enjoy Him in all His marvelous aspects in 1 Corinthians. The concluding aspect in this book is that Christ is the life-giving Spirit. When we call, "O Lord

Jesus," we enjoy the Triune God and all our problems are solved.

After I saw this matter, I began to minister to the saints in a different way. The wives or the husbands came to visit me with problems, and they asked me what to do. I told them that they simply needed to call, "O Lord Jesus." I charged them that they needed to learn to say, "O Lord Jesus, O Lord Jesus." Some asked me what they should do about their bad temper. I told them that when they are going to lose their temper, they should call, "O Lord Jesus, O Lord Jesus, O Lord Jesus." If we would call upon the Lord's name again and again, our temper would be gone and the joy would come. We practiced calling so much nearly twenty years ago, but today we practice very little. In 1969 when we came to the hall, the meeting was filled with "O Lord Jesus." But today our meetings are full of dumbness. May the Lord recover the "O Lord Jesus" among us. All of us have to learn to say, "O Lord Jesus, O Lord Jesus."

When I was a young believer I was taught that we have to realize that we have been crucified with Christ and reckon ourselves to be dead. I tried to realize that I was crucified with Christ and to reckon that I was dead with Christ, but that did not work. Then I found out what does work. What does work is to say, "O Lord Jesus." When you call on the Lord's name, you will experience His death and His resurrection. During the years around 1969 we gave many messages concerning calling on the name of the Lord. Our homes should be filled with calling on the Lord's name.

I hope that when we go out to baptize people and set up meetings in their homes, we will take the lead to call on the name of the Lord, leading the new ones into calling on the name of the Lord Jesus. This will strengthen, enrich, and establish the home meetings. We all need to do this. The preaching in dead letters does not work. We must believe in the living Spirit, who moves when we call on the name of the Lord Jesus. Whenever we say "Lord Jesus," we have the feeling within that the living Spirit is touching us.

By calling on the Lord's name we enjoy all the items of what He is, and we have a stand, a ground, a base, and a strong support to come to the meeting. When we come to the meeting calling on the Lord's name, we come as a living person full of Christ. If we are those who call on the Lord's name, there will be no need for us to try to think of what to say in the meeting. If we open up our mouth, something of Christ will come out of us. This is the way to have the church meetings. If we all would be those who call on the name of the Lord Jesus again and again day by day, whenever we come together the meeting will be high, living, and a real exhibition of Christ. Hymn #864 declares in the chorus:

> Let us exhibit Christ,
> Let us exhibit Christ;
> We'll bring His surplus to the church
> And thus exhibit Christ.

We need to bring the surplus of Christ to every meeting in order to exhibit Christ. We need to enjoy Christ in our daily life, and come together to exhibit Him.

THE MINISTERS OF THE NEW TESTAMENT IN SECOND CORINTHIANS

Second Corinthians, the eighth book of the New Testament, shows us the ministers of the New Testament. When we enjoy Christ in our daily life, we are constituted with His unsearchable riches. Thus, we become the ministers of the New Testament, who dispense the riches of Christ into others. The Spirit, who is the ultimate expression of the processed Triune God becoming a life-giving Spirit, imparts the divine life, even God Himself, into the believers and apostles, making them ministers of a new covenant, the covenant of life (2 Cor. 3:6). Hence, their ministry is one constituted with the Triune God of life by His life-giving Spirit. All the apostles' works are to carry out this unique ministry of ministering Christ to people for the building up of His Body.

CHAPTER FIVE

THE CHRISTIAN GATHERING

Scripture Reading: Matt. 18:20; 1 Cor. 14:23, 26; Acts 2:46; 5:42; 12:12

THE ENJOYMENT OF CHRIST FOR THE CHURCH MEETINGS

One of the principles of how to have proper meetings for the church life is that we must help people learn to enjoy Christ. Without the enjoyment of Christ, it is difficult to have meetings which are profitable for the church life. What we have, what we are, and what we can do, apart from the enjoyment of Christ, are altogether useless. We should not use anything we have, anything we are, or anything we can do to benefit the church meetings. We must abandon all of this because it is altogether unprofitable for the church meeting.

The only thing worthwhile for the church meeting is Christ Himself, the Christ who has passed through all the processes to become the completed Christ. We must learn to enjoy Him, minister Him, and help others to enjoy Him. Then whenever we come together, we come with something of the Christ we have experienced in our daily life. Only Christ in our experience becoming our enjoyment avails for the Christian meetings.

BEING GATHERED INTO THE NAME OF THE LORD FOR THE ENJOYMENT OF HIS PRESENCE

In God's eternal economy the completed Christ is the center, the factor, for us to have Christian meetings for the church life. In this chapter we must go on to see some of the details of Christian meetings. First, we have to help the new ones in the home meetings realize that Christian meetings are a gathering into the name of the Lord for the enjoyment of His presence (Matt. 18:20). We are not gathered into an organization, a teaching, or a practice. We are gathered into the name of the Lord Jesus. The name of the Lord always denotes His person. A name denotes a real and practical person, and the person of the Lord Jesus is the Spirit. Jesus Christ today is the life-giving Spirit (1 Cor. 15:45b). Second Corinthians 3:17 says, "The Lord is the Spirit."

We must teach and lead all the new ones into the realization that they need to call on the name of the Lord whenever they come to a meeting. The more times they call on the name of the Lord Jesus the better. Neither we nor the new ones should come to the meeting silently, dumbly, without opening our mouths to call on the name of the Lord. Calling, "Lord Jesus, Lord Jesus," will bring life into the meeting and make the meeting atmosphere living, high, and rich. To some extent, we have to train the new believers to call on the Lord's name, saying, "Lord Jesus!" First Corinthians 12:3 says, "No one can say, Lord Jesus, except in the Holy Spirit." This indicates that when we say with a proper spirit, "Lord Jesus," we are in the Holy Spirit. Hence, to call on the Lord Jesus is the way to participate in, to enjoy, and to experience the Holy Spirit.

We must link Matthew 18:20 and 1 Corinthians 12:3 together. First, to meet together is to be gathered into the person of the Lord Jesus, and to be gathered into His person means to be gathered into the Spirit. Second, whenever we come together, regardless of how large or small the gathering is, we must practice to call on the name of the Lord that we may get into the Spirit. When we get into the Spirit, we are in the person of the Lord Jesus. When we are in the person of the Lord Jesus, we are in the reality of the name of the Lord Jesus. If we practice setting up home meetings with this realization, we must first take the lead to call on the name of the Lord for the new believers to follow. If they would not follow, then we must take the lead to call and ask them to follow our example. We should call on the name of the Lord and encourage them to follow our calling on the name. Gradually, they will get into the practice. We must tell them that it is not a small thing to have this practice, because when they call on the name of the Lord, they get into the Spirit, who is the very person of the Lord Jesus.

Matthew 18:20 in the King James Version of the New Testament along with other versions says that two or three are "gathered together in My name." Actually, the preposition "in" is "into" in Greek. We are gathered into the name of the Lord. Before the meeting, we may be occupied with many things. The sisters may be occupied with their children, home affairs, and many anxieties. Thus, when the meeting comes, the Lord Jesus gathers us out of these preoccupations. We then turn our heart to the Lord and call upon the name of the Lord Jesus from deep within our spirit. As a result, we get into the name, the person, the Spirit, of the Lord. In such a Spirit, under such a condition, we have a meeting. We must practice calling on the Lord's name until we are rescued and pulled out of all of our preoccupations.

We should not wait until we enter into the meeting place to call on the Lord Jesus. Before entering the meeting place, whenever we have the thought to go to the meeting, we should begin to call, "O Lord Jesus." While we are driving to the place of meeting, we should start calling, "O Lord Jesus," the earlier the better. When we call on the name, we touch the Lord's person, and His person is the Spirit. Therefore, as we are calling, we are in the Spirit already, even though we have not yet entered the meeting place.

We come together into the reality of the Lord's presence, which is the Spirit. The Spirit is the Lord's person and the Lord's presence. Following the mention of two or three being gathered into the Lord's name in Matthew 18:20, the Lord says, "...there I am in their midst." Thus, we enjoy the presence of the Lord.

We should not go to the meetings silently according to our old custom, habit, or practice. We must forget our old practice. In setting up and holding the meetings with the new believers, we must practice calling on the name of the Lord. First, in our homes, we should start to call on the Lord's name before we go to the meetings. Then on our way to the meeting, we should continue calling on His name.

Arriving at the meeting place, we will be fully in the Spirit; then we can take the initiative to call, and the new believers will take us as their example. They will follow and imitate us. Hence, all the new believers will be the callers. When we come together by calling upon the name of the Lord, we are in a meeting that is a genuine Christian gathering.

CHRISTIAN MEETINGS TO CARRY OUT THE DIVINE ECONOMY

The Building Up of the Church

First Corinthians is the unique book regarding Christian meetings (11:17; 14:23, 26, 34, 35) revealing that the Christian meetings are to build up the church (14:4-5, 12, 26). We should keep this thought in our understanding whenever we take the lead to help the home meetings. Our purpose is not just to save sinners or to edify the new believers. Our ultimate purpose, our final goal, is to build up the church. From the beginning, we must have this understanding, and with this understanding we will impress people. Whatever we are will impress people. If you are a happy person, your happy face will impress people. If you are a sad person, your sad face and sad appearance will impress people. We must learn to impress people by what we are, what we think, and what we understand. What we understand is that we are here to build up the church. Our standing is to build up the church. Thus, in every kind of activity, whether preaching the gospel, edifying the saints, or going to the meetings, our goal is to build up the church.

Many times we do not need to mention the term church. We should simply do whatever we do with the realization of the building up of the church. Then whatever we do, whatever we say, and whatever we are, will impress people, and all of the new ones will be brought into this same realization concerning the building up of the church.

Building the Church by the Spirit's Gifts, the Lord's Ministries, and God's Operations

We build up the church in the church meetings by the

THE CHRISTIAN GATHERING

Spirit's gifts, the Lord's ministries, and God's operations (1 Cor. 12:3-7). We enjoy the Spirit's gifts by enjoying Christ and, following our enjoyment of Christ, we call upon His name. During our day, in our daily life, we need to enjoy Christ all the time. Then we need to practice calling on the name of the Lord according to what we have enjoyed of the Lord. By these two things we will have the gift.

The gift comes out of the growth in life, and the growth in life comes out of our enjoyment of Christ. If we do not enjoy Christ, there is no growth in Him. However, the more we enjoy Him as our life supply, the more we grow in life, and the more we grow in life, the more the gift is produced. The gift is an issue of the enjoyment of Christ. This is different from the so-called Pentecostal teaching, but it is completely according to the Bible's revelation. The so-called Pentecostal gift that comes suddenly does not last long. There is the need of the gift as an issue of the growth in life. When there is the growth in life, that growth produces a certain gift.

A baby boy has very little gift because there is little growth in life. He needs some measure of growth in life which develops his gift. As he grows day after day, month after month, and year after year, the growth in life brings the gift. He begins to speak, crawl, stand, and walk. These are all gifts brought in through the growth in life. Growth brings the gift. We must help the new believers to enjoy Christ, to grow in Christ, and by this growth and calling on the name of the Lord, the gifts will be produced. When the gifts are produced, the new believers simply need to function. When they function, they accomplish the Lord's ministries by preaching the gospel to save sinners and by ministering life to edify the saints for the building up of the church life. The result is not just that sinners are saved or saints are edified but that the church is built up.

The Spirit's gifts, the Lord's ministries, and the operation of God should be manifested among all the attendants in the meetings, including the meetings of the new believers. Therefore, we do not go to a new believers' meeting and only teach them to pray or teach them with the *Life Lessons* or *Truth Lessons*. This alone is inadequate. We must be a person who enjoys Christ daily; then as we take the lead among the new believers, they will follow us to enjoy Christ. We must become callers, learning to call on the name of the Lord Jesus all the time. As callers, we set up an example for the new ones, and they too will follow us to call on the Lord's name. As they call, they will get into the Spirit. Then whenever we come together with them, the gifts will be manifested among them and the functions will follow. Thus, the operation of God will be accomplished.

GOD'S ORDAINED WAY FOR CHRISTIAN MEETINGS

God's ordained way for Christian meetings is to have two different sizes of meetings: small and large. The smaller size is to be held or practiced in the believers' homes. Do not despise the small meetings. You may only meet with another couple or with parents and their little child. Apparently, such a small meeting seems insignificant. But you have to realize that human society is composed of small homes with small families. A community or society of millions of people comes from small families. No human society can be built up without the small families in their small homes. In human society big gatherings are not held that regularly. Instead the husband, wife, and children come together in their own home every day. If every family is strong, the community and society will be strong.

In the past we followed Christianity's way to esteem the big meetings. When we held big meetings, we felt good and happy, and we felt that we had something of which to boast. But when we had a small meeting of only three or four persons, we were disappointed. Within the last year in Taipei, however, nearly three thousand new home meetings have been established. Each home meeting is composed of about three or four. If you look at a single home meeting, it seems that it is too small and insignificant. But when you put them all together, they mean a great deal.

In the Believers' Homes

The believers first met in the homes beginning on the day of Pentecost (Acts 2:46). Three thousand met from house to house. The Greek indicates that they met according to houses, which means that every house had a meeting. There was a meeting in every new believer's house. This could only happen by the Spirit. Furthermore, there were many calling on the name of the Lord (Acts 2:21).

In the home meetings, according to Acts 2:46 and 5:42, there were preaching the gospel, teaching the truth, breaking bread to remember the Lord, and prayers. The saints around the time of Pentecost broke bread every day, that is, they had the remembrance of the Lord by practicing the Lord's table. The saints also prayed in their homes. Acts 12:12 tells us that when Peter was released from prison, he went to the house of Mary where a group of saints were praying.

Meeting in the believers' homes is for all the members of Christ to function. In any big meeting it is hard for the saints to function. But in a small meeting with four or five, or two or three, even a small boy or girl could function. He or she could say, "The Lord Jesus loves me, and it is so good that I love Him." This is a small function, but do not despise it. The new believers will function in a small way at first, but from that point, they will continue to progress in life and in function. By the functioning of all the members, the small home meetings will grow and be built up. When a new couple brings forth a little infant, they have the faith that their family will be built up. The same applies to the home meetings. We should exercise our faith and practice the home meetings with much expectation.

In Matthew 18:20, in speaking about Christian gatherings, the Lord Jesus used the number of two or three: "For where two or three are gathered together into My name, there I am in their midst." Two or three is a precious number in the Bible, and should be the starting number of the church life. When the church becomes big through the home meetings, the big meetings will be meaningful. But when the church does not have anything and expects to have a big meeting, that big meeting may be empty. To start the church life from a small meeting of two or three is best.

All of us like to start a meeting with a lot of people, yet the more people you have as a start in a meeting, the more trouble you will suffer. In 1949 when we began the ministry on the island of Taiwan, we called a conference. On the firstLord's day morning, close to four hundred came. Most of them were newcomers who had just come from mainland China. They were Christians who did not have a place to worship, so when they heard about the gathering at the meeting hall, they came. When I looked at the number, I realized that it was too many, so I immediately gave a message saying, "The church here does not help people in marriage, nor does it help people get jobs, nor does it help people financially. The church here only preaches Christ and ministers Christ to people as their life supply. If you are seeking after Christ you are the right person to come here. Otherwise, you have the wrong place."

I then gave an illustration about the different kinds of restaurants among the Chinese people. There are the Shanghainese who like to eat Shanghai food and the Cantonese who like to eat Canton food. Different Christian assemblies stress different things like different restaurants. If you are Shanghainese and go to a Cantonese restaurant, you will feel that you are in the wrong place, because you cannot get the Shanghai food. Then I told them again, "The church here does not help people in marriage, finance, or employment. We only help people to know the Lord Jesus, receive Him, and enjoy Him. If you are such a person, you have come to the right place. Please continue to come." After I gave that message, half of the number returned for the next meeting. I said to myself, "These are the genuine ones seeking after Christ Himself." When the saints recorded the names, there were nearly two hundred. This number formed the start of the church life in Taiwan. To begin the church life with a lesser number is better. Do not despise the small meetings. In these small meetings, we should preach the gospel, teach the truth, break bread to remember the Lord, pray, and give the opportunity for each attendant to function.

In a Larger Meeting Place

The church should also have large meetings in a larger place for the whole church to come together (1 Cor. 14:23). There are two kinds of meetings: small meetings in the homes of the believers and large meetings in a larger meeting place. These large meetings should not be held often. To have these larger meetings should not be a constant practice. If you practice the large meetings constantly, you will deaden the situation. You must learn to have the two kinds of meetings.

We must be balanced. God's design of our body is symmetrical. We have two ears, two eyes, two nostrils, two lips, two shoulders, two arms, two hands, two thighs, two legs, and two feet. On the one hand, we need to begin the meeting in small homes; on the other hand, when the need arises we should hold large meetings in a larger meeting place. In the larger meeting place, we should not have any definite speaker with all the congregation listening to this speaker. We must kill this practice. In such a meeting all the attendants should participate in the building up of the church through their functions (1 Cor. 14:26). When we come together one may have a revelation, another may have a hymn, another one may have a teaching, and others may have another portion. Everyone can and should have something of Christ for the meeting. We all need to have something so that we can function in the meetings for the building up of the church.

No Chairman, No Leaders, and No Formalities

In both the small and large meetings there should be no chairman, no leaders, and no formalities. This will annul Christianity. If the chairman, leaders, and formalities are taken away from Christianity, there is nothing left. In every meeting all the attendants should participate. They can pray, offer some praise to God, call a hymn, take the lead to sing a hymn, read the Scriptures, or give a testimony. This makes the meeting different from Christianity. By practicing to give time and opportunity to all the attendants to function, all the saints may render their help, and the entire church will get the benefit (1 Cor. 14:26, 31).

CHAPTER SIX

THE SUPPORT OF THE CHURCH MEETINGS

Scripture Reading: Phil. 1:20-21; 1 Cor. 14:26; Eph. 4:15-16

THE CHRISTIAN DAILY LIFE—TO LIVE CHRIST

For anything to exist, to act, and to live, there must be a support for that thing. We have seen that the church life depends upon the church meetings. The church meetings are very crucial to the church life. In this chapter we want to fellowship concerning the support of the church meetings. The support of the church meetings is the Christian daily life—to live Christ (Phil. 1:20-21). The Christian daily life is not just a matter of good behavior or character. The Bible reveals clearly that the Christian daily life is nothing less than Christ Himself. Christ Himself should be our daily life. In China there were a number of people who practiced according to the teaching of Confucius, and their behavior and character were very commendable. However, they did not have the Christian daily life because they did not have Christ as their life and as their living. They did not have Christ as their everything in their human life. They might have had good character, but they did not have the Christian daily life.

To have good meetings, the support is not merely good character. The support must be Christ Himself lived out of us. The new way stresses the Christian meeting, and the Christian meeting needs such a support of a daily life in which Christ Himself is lived out of us. Only Christ, the living One, can capture people. When we go to visit people by knocking on their doors, we must be linked to this living Christ. We should not only live for Him or to Him but also live Him. He is our life within, and He is our living without. We need to live Him daily.

To live Him means first to take Him as our life. As regenerated persons, we should take Him as our life.

Though we have a natural life, a human life, a life created by God, that life is not the divine life. The human life was created by God to contain the divine life. Genesis 1 tells us that God created man in His own image (v. 26). Genesis 2 records that God put this man in front of the tree of life, indicating that this created human being needed the divine life (vv. 7-9). When we believe into Christ, He comes into us not only to be our Savior but even the more to be our life, thus fulfilling the purpose of God. The Lord Jesus said that He was the life (John 14:6), and Paul said that Christ is our life (Col. 3:4). Thus, Paul also said that to him to live was Christ (Phil. 1:21). We must live Christ, not just live for Christ or to Christ. Christ is our life and our life supply, and Christ should be our living, our very expression.

To live Christ is the Christian daily life, and this supports the Christian meetings. If we come to a meeting without such a living, such a daily life, we come in an empty and a dead way. Without such a living we could never support the Christian meeting. Regardless of how zealous we might be, we could never impart Christ into people as their life or life supply. We must live Christ. Day after day Christ should be our living.

To have such a living we must learn to deny ourself. God has no intention for us to live, but His only intention is for us to take Christ into us to replace our life so that He can be our very life. This should not be just a teaching to us; this should be our daily practice. Among us in the Lord's recovery, I have noticed through the years that not too many saints really practice denying the self and taking Christ as their life. We must deny ourselves. When we love a person, we have to love that person by denying ourself and taking Christ as our love. We should let Christ love people through us. We should let Christ's love become our love with which we love others. The Christian life is not a matter of us loving people but a matter of Christ loving people from within us. What comes out of us should not be our natural human love but Christ Himself.

When we talk to people, we must learn to deny ourself

and take Christ as our life to express Christ. We should not talk with people by ourself. We must learn and practice to talk to people by denying ourself. Not only daily but also moment by moment, we must practice to do things, to live, to act, and to have our being in Christ, with Christ, and by Christ. We should also learn how to walk by praying to Him all the time (1 Thes. 5:17). While we are going to work, we have to go by praying. The best way to pray unceasingly is to call on the name of the Lord. While you are taking the cross, you have to do it by calling as a kind of instant and unceasing prayer to the Lord. To call on the Lord's name is to breathe in Christ (Lam. 3:55-57). Whenever you say "O Lord Jesus," you really breathe Christ into you.

When the Lord's recovery came to the United States, a brother who had been a preacher turned this way. One day I called Hymn #255 by A. B. Simpson. The chorus of this hymn says:

> I am breathing out my sorrow,
> Breathing out my sin;
> I am breathing, breathing, breathing,
> All Thy fullness in.

After we sang that hymn this brother did not understand what A. B. Simpson was talking about, and he told me he did not like this song. A number of years later pray-reading the Word and calling on the name of the Lord Jesus came into the Lord's recovery, and this brother practiced these things. One day I met him in another city and he told me, "Brother Lee, to me the best hymn is #255 on breathing."

Without breathing, we all would soon expire. Our calling on the name of the Lord is breathing and is an instant and unceasing prayer. By calling we can pray unceasingly, and by this kind of prayer we actually and spontaneously take Christ as our life. Then we do things by Him and not by ourselves. We talk to people by Him and not by ourselves. Calling on His name causes us to live Christ, to have a proper Christian daily life. If we are such persons who practice calling on the Lord daily, we will come together full of Christ, with a living, rejoicing spirit. The meeting will not be vacant, empty, or idle. Instead the meeting will be busy, full of spiritual activities by members who live Christ daily. The meeting will be so high, so rich, so fresh, and so refreshing.

The fellowship in this book is not for the purpose of giving us more doctrine and teachings. What we are fellowshipping is altogether for us to practice. From today, we all should exercise to practice the New Testament economy. I have noticed that even during our trainings, the trainees were in the heavens as they were listening to the messages. But in between the meetings they became "people under the earth." They were no longer people in the heavens. This shows us that we must practice to live Christ not only in the ministry meetings but also in our daily life. A husband should talk to his wife by Christ, and a wife should talk to her husband by Christ. We should talk by taking Christ. In our talking to our spouse we should live Christ. We need to mean business to really take Him as our life and live Him. Then we will be the right persons to come to the meetings, and with such a daily life, we will become a strong support. Even if only five saints out of one hundred meeting together would be persons who exercise to take Christ as their life and live Him, that meeting would be very fresh and very refreshing.

THE CHRISTIAN DAILY LIFE FOR THE CHURCH LIFE

The Christian daily life is for the church life. We Christians live Christ as our daily life for the church testimony. The church as Christ's Body is Christ Himself (1 Cor. 12:12). Anyone's body is himself. If we do not have a body, we do not have an expression. Our body is our being's expression. As the members of the Body of Christ, the church, we should live Christ. If we do not live Christ, we are His members in name, but not in practicality. The matter of living Christ has not been taken into our practice. Even many elders do not practice to live Christ. Many elders practice behaving. They try not to make a mistake. They try not to be wrong and always to be right. They are always correcting themselves. Humanly speaking, this is very good but there is no Christ in their behavior.

Many of our church meetings are cold, old, poor, and dead because many of the saints are behaving believers. They behave well, but they do not live Christ as their daily life. Thus, among them there is no real church life. The church is just a name with them, and the church life is just a term with them. Many of the saints try to do the right things, and many of the leading ones in the local churches practice behaving instead of living Christ as the reality of their daily life. Many leading ones are afraid of doing anything wrong or of making a mistake. They feel that as long as they are right and correct, everything is okay. But we need to realize that good behavior in itself is not okay. If all of us are merely good people who behave well, then the church becomes a social club. In the church life we should practice Christ, not behavior. Christ must be our life, our essence, our being, our living, our existing, and our everything. We should practice Christ all the time. Christ can never be wrong. He is always good. But the point in living Christ is not to be right, but to express Christ. What we should express is not a certain kind of behavior or character. For the proper church life we need to express Christ Himself. The proper church life depends upon the church meeting in a living way with everybody living Christ.

THE CHURCH MEETINGS BEING THE EXHIBITIONS OF THE CHRISTIAN DAILY LIFE

The church meetings are the exhibitions of the Christian daily life. Whenever we come together, we have an exhibition. We do not come together to exhibit our ability, our wisdom, our behavior, our goodness, or our morality. We come together to exhibit Christ. If we do not live Christ daily, we have no Christ to exhibit in the church meetings. In 1961 when I was in Taipei, I wrote the hymn that says, "Let us exhibit Christ" (*Hymns*, #864). A few years later this hymn was translated into English, and it helped many of the saints. But the saints did not receive the help from this hymn to live Christ in their daily life (see verses 2 and 3). It mostly helped them to practice living Christ in the meetings. Formerly, they stood up in the meetings to say something to express their goodness, their kindness, their humility, or their patience. Then they learned to speak something of Christ, and not of themselves, in the meetings. Thus, the meetings changed, yet that change could not last long. For the long run, if we do not experience Christ daily, we will have nothing to say of Christ. If we do not live Christ in our daily life, we will become empty. Then we will only be able to repeat old stories in the church meetings. If we only exercise when we come together to meet, there may be a little expression of Christ in the church meeting, but no expression of Christ in our daily life. We may be good people without much of Christ in our daily living. Thus, when we come to the meeting, we are still poor in the experience of Christ.

Now that we are going to set up home meetings with new believers, we must be persons living Christ all day. What we are we minister to people, and what we live we minister to people. We must preach what we live and teach what we are by having Christ. Otherwise, we are just actors. An actor is one who does not live in the way that he acts in the theater. We should not be actors in the church meetings. Whatever we do must be the same as what we live in our daily life. In our daily life we live Christ, so we come to the meeting and still exhibit Christ. Then the meeting is a genuine exhibition of Christ.

When you come to the new believers to meet with them as a person full of Christ, spontaneously whatever you say, pray, or sing expresses Christ. Even your smile will express Christ and give people the impression that you are a man of Christ. You will be found by the new believers in Christ. Paul said that he was seeking to be found in Christ (Phil. 3:9), and we need to be found by others in Christ. To be found in Christ is not a matter of outward behavior. You may try to behave like a person in Christ, but this resembles a monkey behaving like a man. It is not genuine. We must live Christ every moment in every small

THE SUPPORT OF THE CHURCH MEETINGS   63

detail. Then Christ will be constituted into our being to be our spiritual constitution. People will find us in Christ in whatever we say or do. Our being such persons will help the new believers to have living home meetings. To hold a home meeting is not a matter of just bringing techniques to the new ones, of teaching them how to call a hymn, sing a hymn, read the Bible, or give a testimony. The home meeting is to exhibit what we are in our daily life. We must live Christ in our daily life. We must be men in Christ, men always found by people in Christ. Then our meeting will be full of Christ. Only Christ is the living One, and only He can make a meeting alive, full of life. We must stress living Christ and practice to live Christ.

LIVING CHRIST TO SPREAD THE GOSPEL

Our going out to visit people by knocking on their doors is a wonderful, proven practice. I received letters from some saints, however, who told me that they knocked on doors for a long time without getting any baptized. Surely such a person would be thoroughly disappointed and say that door knocking does not work. But door knocking does work, and it has been proven for over two years in Taipei. Others have said that to visit people by knocking on their doors will only work in Taiwan and not anywhere else. The statistics of our going out to visit others in the 1987 summer training here in Anaheim, however, prove that the rate of increase here is about the same as, and even higher than, in Taipei. Our success depends upon whether or not we have been trained in the Lord's new way. Door knocking works, but you may not have been trained. You may not be successful because you have not practiced strictly what the training has discovered in the recent past. Those who have been trained to visit people, to baptize them, and to establish home meetings can testify that the trained way works. The churches in the United States need the training.

When we get into the training and practice it strictly, we will be addicted to visiting others. If you baptize three new ones in one evening, you will be "crazy." The first baptism makes you happy, the second one will shock you, and the third one will make you crazy with enjoyment. Then you will look forward to going out again. In the training meetings in Taipei a number of saints testified that they became addicted to door knocking and could not wait for another evening to go out. When you get into the enjoyment of door knocking, door knocking is more prevailing. Door knocking does not work with you when you are so dead and cold. However, when you are crazy with enjoyment in a proper way, every home that you visit is touched by you. It is not the doors that we knock on that make a difference but the person who knocks on them. When you pray for fifteen minutes with your team before going out and become happy in the Lord and crazy in the enjoyment of Christ, the doors that you knock on will open to you. Not only will the doors open, but also the people behind these doors will have open hearts to believe and open mouths to call on the name of the Lord and to pray and will be ready to be baptized.

Many times when the saints went out to preach the gospel, a person believed within five minutes and within another five minutes he was baptized. These were saved in a living way. We do not baptize people in a cold, silent, and dead way. The ones that we baptize get baptized calling on the name of the Lord in a living way (Acts 22:16). Sometimes in Taipei while the saints were preaching to the husband, the wife went into the bathroom to prepare the water for baptism although she had not yet believed. Baptism is an expression of the miracle of faith. Faith brings Christ into us. To ask a new believer to wait for a certain day to be baptized is wrong and unscriptural. The Bible tells us to believe and be baptized, not to believe and wait for a certain period of time until the church has a baptism. There is not such a record in the book of Acts. If we want to be prevailing persons in visiting people, we must be crazy with the enjoyment of Christ and happy in the Lord. If we are crazy in such a way, doors will be opened, hearts will be opened, mouths will be opened, and people will receive the Lord and be baptized. It is a miracle to save a person. No good philosophy or ethical teaching can save people in this way. When we Christians become crazy in Christ, we can do miracles. Thus, we have to live Christ every day. The more we live Him, the more we are crazy in Him.

THE CHURCH MEETINGS PROMOTING, STRENGTHENING, IMPROVING, AND ENRICHING THE CHRISTIAN DAILY LIFE

The church meetings promote, strengthen, improve, and enrich the Christian daily life. If Christ is making you crazy, that is, if you are living Christ every day and coming to the meeting with Christ and full of Christ, you will have a good meeting. This good meeting will promote, strengthen, improve, and enrich your Christian daily life.

A CYCLE FOR THE CHRISTIANS' GROWTH WITH CHRIST FOR THE BUILDING UP OF THE BODY OF CHRIST

Eventually, the Christian daily life and the church meetings become a cycle for the Christians' growth with Christ for the building up of the Body of Christ (1 Cor. 14:26; Eph. 4:15-16). We go out to knock on doors to get people baptized and set up meetings in their homes not merely to save them or release the truth to them. Our burden is to regenerate them to be the members of Christ, and eventually through the home meetings, they all will be built up as the living Body of Christ. We need to build up the Body of Christ according to the God-ordained way to carry out the New Testament economy. The fellowship in this chapter needs to be brought into our practice so that we have a church-supporting daily life, which is Christ living in us and lived out of us.

Chapter Seven

THE BASIC FACTORS FOR THE CHRISTIAN MEETINGS

(1)

Scripture Reading: Rom. 8:11; 2 Tim. 1:7; Eph. 5:18b; 1 Cor. 6:17; Acts 13:52; Gal. 5:16, 25; 1 Cor. 14:15; Eph. 6:18

THE BELIEVERS' SPIRIT AND THE SPIRIT

According to the Bible and to our experience there are four basic factors for the Christian meetings: the mingled spirit, the word, praying, and singing. The first basic factor is the mingled spirit. In many verses in the New Testament, especially in Romans 8 and Galatians 5, whether the word spirit refers to the Holy Spirit or to the human spirit is difficult to discern. Such a spirit in these verses is the mingled spirit. The Holy Spirit indwells and mingles Himself with our regenerated spirit (Rom. 8:16; cf. 1 Cor. 6:17).

The human, God-created spirit of the unbelievers is not regenerated, but as Christians, our spirit has been regenerated (John 3:6). To be regenerated means to have God's life imparted into our spirit. When God the Spirit regenerates us, He imparts God Himself as the divine life into our being, that is, into our spirit. The unbelievers' spirit has no divine element, but our spirit does have the divine element because the life of God has been imparted and added into our spirit. The great difference between the believers' spirit and the unbelievers' spirit is that we have the divine life as the divine element in our spirit. Because the divine life has been imparted into our human spirit, we may say that our human spirit has been made divine.

In our regenerated spirit, not only do we have the divine life but we also have the Holy Spirit (Rom. 8:16). This Spirit is the very consummation of the Triune God. The

Father is the source, the Son is the course, and the Spirit is the consummation of the divine Trinity. The divine Trinity is one, yet He has these three aspects: the source, the course, and the consummation. The Spirit of God is the consummation of the Triune God to reach us. Without the Spirit of God, God cannot reach us. If there were no Holy Spirit, Christ could only come to us to stay among us; He could not get into us. In order to get into us, He had to become the life-giving Spirit (1 Cor. 15:45b). This life-giving Spirit is the breath of life. On the day of resurrection, when Christ came back in the evening to His disciples, He breathed Himself into them, and He called what was breathed into them the Holy Spirit (John 20:22). This strongly indicates that the resurrected Christ, the pneumatic Christ, is the life-giving Spirit as the breath breathed into all His believing ones. Now the Holy Spirit is in the believers' spirit in addition to the divine life.

The believers' spirit is a composition of three things: our human spirit, the divine life, and the Holy Spirit. Our spirit is now a compound spirit, which is the mingled spirit. The Holy Spirit has mingled Himself with our human spirit in the element of the divine life. It is difficult to see much growth in life among many Christians because very few know about this mingled spirit with the divine life as the mingling element. We cannot have the growth in life if we do not know the mingled spirit in the element of the divine life.

The believers' spirit is indwelt by the Spirit (Rom. 8:11). The Spirit is not only in us and remains within us, but He dwells in us. To dwell is to settle down. When we stay in a hotel, we only lodge there for awhile, but we do not dwell there. But when we own a house, we settle in it, that is, we dwell in it. The Holy Spirit does not merely lodge in our spirit but He dwells or settles down in our spirit. The Holy Spirit indwelling our spirit is a wonderful fact.

Our spirit should be living, fresh, strong, and active. Second Timothy 1:7 says that God has not given us a spirit of cowardice, but of power and of love and of a sober mind. Love refers to affection, power refers to strength, and a sober mind means that we think and behave with a restricted and sober understanding. In order for our spirit, the spirit indwelt by the Holy Spirit, to be fresh, strong, and active, we must exercise our spirit.

The believers' spirit is also filled with God as the Spirit and filled with the pneumatic Christ (Eph. 5:18b). Although God, the pneumatic Christ, is within us, we need to be filled with Him. In the New Testament, to be filled implies saturation. God is within us as the pneumatic Christ both filling and saturating us. We must learn how to realize the infilling, the saturating, of the divine Trinity. The mingling starts within our spirit, and the saturating carries out the mingling through our entire being, from our spirit through our soul to our body. The Lord saturates us with Himself by filling us up. We need much experience of the mingled spirit, of its infilling and its saturating. Then we will be saturated with the Triune God. The water in a cup can fill the cup, but it cannot saturate the cup. But we as human beings can be saturated by the indwelling God. All the parts of our soul and all the parts of our body need to be saturated with the Triune God so that we can be constituted into God-men.

The believers' spirit is one with the Spirit. First Corinthians 6:17 says, "But he who is joined to the Lord is one spirit." How wonderful that we human beings can become one spirit with the Lord! The Lord is the Spirit, He created us with a spirit, He regenerated our spirit, and He indwells our spirit. Now our spirit is joined to His Spirit, and the two spirits are one spirit. We, the believers of Christ, who love Him and who would let Him do everything to saturate us thoroughly, have become one spirit with Him. The experience of being one spirit with the Lord is real and practical. Quite often, before I was to speak, I prayed, "Lord, grant me the grace to practice being one spirit with You, and vindicate the fact that You are one spirit with me in my speaking." The greatest miracle in the universe is that human beings with flesh and blood can be one spirit with the Triune God. God's salvation is many times higher than any philosophy. All philosophies attempt to develop our mind, our psychology, our *psuche* life, which is merely to develop the "poor me." But regardless of how much you develop yourself, you are still yourself. God's salvation is not to develop our mind but to put Himself into our being, to have His element saturating our being to make our being one with His divine life. To enjoy this salvation we need to practice being one spirit with the Lord.

THE SUSTAINING AND STRENGTHENING FACTOR FOR THE CHRISTIAN MEETING

The way to practice being one spirit with the Lord is to call on His name unceasingly. Do not call on the Lord only before the meeting, after the meeting, or in the meeting. You have to call, "O Lord Jesus," all the time. This will always keep you in the element of the divine mingling. Then, in all that you do and say, you will act as a person being one spirit with the Lord. You will not simply be a good person, a person full of proper character and ethical morality. You will be a person full of God. God will be expressed and manifested through you.

The mingled spirit is a strong, basic factor of the Christian meeting. Who comes to the Christian meeting, you or God? It should be that both you and God come in the way of being one spirit. When we come to the meeting with God, we come as a wonderful person, a God-man. When we come, God comes; when God comes, we come. We do not only come together, but we and He come as one spirit. If fifty people met together in this way, that meeting would be glorious.

Sometimes the strong factor of the mingled spirit is not in the meeting. There is nothing of the divine Being to be the very element that sustains the meeting. To have the factor of the mingled spirit in our meetings requires not only our exercise in the meeting but also the practice of being one spirit with the Lord in our daily life to let the divine Being saturate our human being. Then we will come into the meeting as a God-man. You may have come to the meeting in a defeated way apart from God. You may have called a hymn in the meeting, but it was altogether you who did it, not God. When you come into the meeting, God should come with you. When you sing, God should sing. The indwelling Spirit within us must have the full freedom to move and act. We have had many experiences in which we sensed the indwelling Spirit moving in us, yet with little freedom. We give Him too much restriction, and we confine Him. As a result, we may have the divine Trinity in our being, but we do not have the divine Trinity saturating us. When we come to the meeting, it is only we who come and not God. If we do something in the meeting, it is merely we who do it. The meeting is not sustained by our being there.

But if we are persons practicing to be one spirit with the Lord, we will be a strong, sustaining element in the meeting. If there are even three to five such persons among fifty meeting together, that meeting will be very strong because that meeting has some who are the very sustaining essence. They do not necessarily need to speak or to do anything. Even if they just sit there, their presence will sustain the meeting. Often when certain brothers were absent from the meeting, it became weak, empty, and poor. When these brothers come in, their presence brings in the strengthening essence of the mingled spirit. Simply to learn how to set up home meetings in the new believers' homes is not adequate. Your being must be dealt with. Your being must be filled and saturated with the divine element. When you go to the home meetings as such a person, you will sustain the meetings.

In the recent past a certain denomination began to practice meeting in small groups in many saints' homes. When they came together, however, the attendants just sat there without knowing what to do. Even the leader did not know what to do. There was the real absence of the sustaining element in the meeting. If there is little Christ in our daily life and no Spirit in our very being saturating us and making us one spirit with the divine Trinity, our meetings will be empty. Sometimes our meetings have been like this. The meeting may have been scheduled to begin at

7:30 p.m., but by 7:35 p.m. only one person had arrived. Gradually the saints came in one by one. The meeting was deadened, and there was no sustaining essence, that is, no factor of God in the Spirit. The Lord's new way is not just to set up meetings in the homes. We have to have ourselves dealt with by the infilling and the saturating of the divine Trinity.

THE EXERCISE OF THE SPIRIT

We need to exercise our spirit for the church meetings. The way to exercise is to call "O Lord Jesus." Even early in the morning we still can call on the name of the Lord without bothering others. We have to be persons practicing to call on the name of the Lord. Then we have to live by the Spirit (Gal. 5:25a) and walk by the Spirit (Gal. 5:16, 25b). To walk means to have our being, to move, to live, and to do all things. We should have our entire being by the indwelling Spirit, by the mingled spirit. Actually, it is hard to know when we are walking by the Spirit. But if we are not walking by the Spirit, we surely will know it.

Some Christians have strict regulations for their living. One group practices wearing only clothes of a certain color, using mule wagons for transportation, and not using telephones. This kind of practice is a practice without the Spirit. In the New Testament, what God requires is a life with the Spirit. Such a life does not require outward regulations. Once when I was putting on a new tie, the dear Spirit within me bothered me and said, "No." I do not have a pastor to come to approve my tie, but I do have the Spirit to restrict me. If I would wear such a tie against the Spirit's restriction, I would not be able to speak in the meetings. My strength, my secret, my impact, is this bothering Spirit. If I became "divorced" from Him in my daily life, I would be through. The real Christian walk revealed and required by the Bible is to walk by the Spirit and live by the Spirit.

Galatians 5:25 says, "If we live by the Spirit, let us also walk by the Spirit," and 5:16 says, "Walk by the Spirit." To walk by the Spirit in verse 16 differs from to walk by the

Spirit in verse 25b. In verse 16 to walk is to walk in a general way, and in verse 25b to walk is to walk orderly, to walk along a line or by a rule to fulfill a purpose. This indicates that our Christian walk must be a walk generally by the Spirit, and this walk must be also according to the particular rule, that is, to live Christ for the purpose of building up His Body. Galatians 5:16 and 25 show us that the Christian walk must altogether be in this mingling, saturating Spirit, who is one spirit with us. We do not need any outward regulations. When we come to the meeting, we should not care for regulations. We should come in with Him and as Him. When we come, He comes. When we are here, He is here. When we are speaking, He is speaking. To live by the Spirit, walk by the Spirit, pray with the spirit (1 Cor. 14:15a; Eph. 6:18), sing with the spirit (1 Cor. 14:15b), and be strong in the spirit (2 Tim. 1:7) is to exercise the spirit. When we exercise the spirit, the mingled spirit becomes the very factor of the Christian meeting.

In order to exercise our legs, we should walk. If we use our legs all the time, they will become strong. Sometimes when I am sick, I must stay in bed for several days. After three days in bed, my legs become weak. Then I need to walk to recover the strength in my legs. To strengthen our eyes, we need to use our eyes. To strengthen our arm, we need to exercise our arm. Likewise, if we are going to be the sustaining, strengthening factor in the meeting, we need to exercise our spirit all day and every moment, in all things and in all matters. If we go to a home meeting as persons who practice exercising the spirit, we will be a living, strengthening, sustaining, refreshing, supporting, and enriching factor to that meeting. Merely what we say and what we do is not adequate. We must be persons full of the Spirit and saturated with the Spirit to practically become one spirit with the Lord in our daily experience.

CHAPTER EIGHT

THE BASIC FACTORS FOR THE CHRISTIAN MEETINGS

(2)

Scripture Reading: Col. 3:16; Eph. 6:17-18; 1 Cor. 12:8; 14:6, 26

LOGOS AND *RHEMA*

In chapter seven we saw that the first basic factor for the Christian meetings is the mingled spirit. In this chapter we want to fellowship concerning the word as the second basic factor. The word for the Christian meetings is not our word, but the holy word, God's word, the divine word. The two classifications of the word in the New Testament are *logos* and *rhema*. The Greek word *logos* refers to the constant word (Col. 3:16). What is revealed and written in the holy Scriptures is the constant word, the written word, the remaining word, the word that stands for eternity. The Greek word *rhema* refers to the instant word (Eph. 6:17). Anyone who is literate can read the Bible according to its written letter. By reading the Bible, we can receive the constant word of God. The constant word, however, is not so powerful, living, working, energizing, or operating within us until it becomes the instant word. When the constant word becomes the instant word, it becomes living, and it works or operates to accomplish God's purpose in us and with us. Therefore, we must first learn to acquire the constant word and look to the Lord for Him to change His constant word into the instant word. In other words, we should pray when we come to the Bible that God would change His *logos* into *rhema*.

When I was young, I was taught to recite John 3:16. I loved that verse very much, yet that verse was merely a constant word to me for many years. Although I knew and loved that verse, it did not do any work within me, and it had not become a part of my being. One day, however, John 3:16, as the constant word, became the instant word to me. God's word in that verse was applied to my being in a personal way. I realized that God not only loved the world but that He also loved me so much that He gave His only begotten Son, and because I believed in Him, I would not perish but have eternal life. The constant word in John 3:16 had become the instant word to me. It became living and operating within me, and I began to enjoy God in His giving of His Son to me. If we merely read the Bible as the constant word, we will only get some objective knowledge that will not touch our inward being. We need to learn to turn the written and printed word of the Bible into the instant word. In our direct contact with God, the written word is made so practical and that written word becomes the living word. The *logos*, the constant word, will become the *rhema*, the instant word. When the *logos* becomes the *rhema*, we receive the benefit of the Triune God infusing Himself through His living word into our being.

THE WORD OF WISDOM

For the Christian meetings we also need the word of wisdom. The word of wisdom (1 Cor. 12:8a) is concerning Christ as the deeper things of God predestined by God for our portion (1 Cor. 1:24, 30; 2:6-10). We need God's wisdom to understand the revelation of Christ as our God-designated portion. In 1984 I gave a series of messages that are now contained in the book entitled *God's New Testament Economy* (published by Living Stream Ministry). I consider what is presented in that volume as the consummation of what the Lord has shown us in His recovery. The chart of God's New Testament economy on pages 12 and 13 of that book contains many new titles, terms, and phrases. These are words of wisdom. These words are not of human thought, human composition, or human terminology. The words of wisdom come through the revelation of God.

First Corinthians 1:30 tells us that Christ "became

wisdom to us from God: both righteousness and sanctification and redemption." To understand the four terms of wisdom, righteousness, sanctification, and redemption, we need much wisdom. We also need the wisdom to speak the reality of these terms to others. Chapter two of 1 Corinthians tells us that Christ is the depths of God, the deep things of God (v. 10). Christ as the deep things of God is our wisdom. Christ became wisdom to us from God as three vital things in God's salvation: He is our righteousness for our past, our sanctification for our present, and our redemption for our future. The deep things of God are Christ as wisdom to us. We need the wisdom from God's revelation to understand how Christ becomes our righteousness, our sanctification, and our redemption. After talking about these items in chapter one, Paul tells us in chapter two that to understand the deep things of God and to speak or communicate these things to one another, we need the wisdom by the Spirit's revelation (vv. 6-10, 13). The word of wisdom is mainly of our spirit through revelation (1 Cor. 14:26). The word of wisdom is not merely related to our mentality, our understanding. This word is mainly of our spirit through revelation, so we need to pray for the Spirit's enlightening and unveiling.

THE WORD OF KNOWLEDGE

The word of knowledge (1 Cor. 12:8b) imparts the general knowledge of things concerning God and the Lord (8:1-7). The word of knowledge speaks in a general way about the Lord Jesus' dying for us, His accomplishing redemption for us, and His relationship with us. The word of knowledge conveys the things concerning God and concerning Christ the Lord in a general way. First Corinthians 8:1-7 is an illustration of the word of knowledge. The word of knowledge is mainly of our understanding through teaching (1 Cor. 14:26). When I read a portion of the word to someone with some explanation and definition to impart some knowledge to him through my teaching, my word is a word of knowledge.

The deeper and higher word is the word of wisdom; the

shallower and lower word is the word of knowledge. The word of knowledge, however, is also a help as a basic factor for the Christian meetings. Many times we get the word of knowledge in our understanding first. Then when we pray, contact God, talk to God, this word of knowledge may become the word of wisdom.

REVELATION, KNOWLEDGE, AND TEACHING, ALL OF THE WORD, BEING NEEDED IN THE CHURCH MEETINGS

Revelation, knowledge, and teaching, all of the word, are needed in the church meetings (1 Cor. 14:6). We need the word of knowledge and the word of teaching, but we must eventually have the word of revelation. The word of knowledge and the word of teaching may become the word of revelation. To get the word of knowledge is superficial. To get the word of revelation, the word of wisdom, is deeper. Thus, we need to contact the Lord more, to stay with the Lord for a longer time. By our staying with the Lord, our spirit will be exercised. Then the word which we know in our understanding will become the word in our spirit, the word of wisdom. This word will minister life to us, bring light to us, and bring the divine energy into our spiritual being. We have to learn to know the word of knowledge and the word of teaching and let these words become the words of wisdom in our spirit. When the word becomes the word of wisdom in our spirit, it is spirit and life (John 6:63). What we read in the Bible may just remain in our being as the word of knowledge and the word of teaching. But if we would spend more time in the presence of the Lord, this word will become the word of wisdom in our spirit to be our very life supply.

THE BELIEVERS BEING FILLED WITH AND SOAKED IN THE WORD

As believers, we need to be filled with and soaked in the word. Colossians 3:16a says that we need to let the word of Christ dwell in us richly. We need to receive the word of God into us as drinking water to be filled with the word, and we need to dive into the word as bathing water to be soaked in the word. When we are filled with and soaked in the word, we are completely one with the word. Within and without we have the word. We need to be fully wrapped up with the word, soaked with the word outwardly and saturated with the word inwardly. This soaking and filling will make us one with the word to be a man of God's word.

THE WORD BECOMING THE BELIEVERS' SINGING

The word also needs to become the believers' singing (Col. 3:16b). The word should become our song or our hymn. We do not necessarily need to have a written melody to sing the word. We can make a natural, spontaneous melody. We need to sing the word according to our own melody. If we could get a melody for the word, that would be better. But when we spend time to get a melody, that may kill our enjoyment. When the word is revealed within us as the word of wisdom, we will be happy, and we need to sing this word. We do not have to be melodious singers in order to sing the word. We can make a joyful noise unto the Lord (Psa. 100:1) and rejoice in the Lord by singing His word.

PRAY-READING THE WORD

We also need to pray-read the word (Eph. 6:17-18). Pray-reading was a term invented by us to describe the practice of reading the word of God by prayer and with prayer. Our spiritual dictionary has been broadened to include this word. When something is invented in a culture, there is the need of a new word. The unabridged dictionaries are much larger than they were fifty years ago. Language goes along with culture. Now that we have been transferred into the kingdom of God, we have a spiritual culture, a Christian culture. We need the term of pray-reading to match the reality in our Christian culture.

Many saints pray-read throughout church history, but they did not have the term pray-reading. Many of us pray-read the word without any realization of what we were doing. After we got saved, we may have read a verse that was so inspiring and pleasing to us. Spontaneously, we repeated it in the way of praying. Andrew Murray was one among many saints who turned God's word into prayer (see *'Lord...Thou Saidst'*, pp. 66-67, published by Living Stream Ministry). Many saints throughout church history pointed out that the best way to understand the word is to read it prayerfully.

To read the word with prayer and by prayer, to pray-read the word, is the best way to read the word. Mere reading only needs our eyes and our understanding, our mentality. But to receive God's word into the depths of our being, our spirit is needed, and the prevailing way to exercise our spirit is by praying. Whenever we pray, we spontaneously exercise our spirit. Then what we read with our eyes and understand in our mentality will go into our spirit through our prayer. Every word in the Bible needs our pray-reading.

HOW TO HANDLE GOD'S WORD

We all need to learn how to handle God's word. The first principle in handling God's word is that we should not exercise our mind too much. Our mind is like a wild horse in need of a bridle. Quite often I received letters from various saints telling me of the "revelations" they have received from the word. Many times their "revelation" is peculiar and off from God's word. When we read the Bible, we have to bridle our "wild horse," our mind. Our mind must be in subjection to our spirit when we get into God's word.

There are many notes in the Recovery Version on the genealogy of Jesus Christ in the first seventeen verses of Matthew 1. In this genealogy of Christ it is significant that five women are mentioned. Only one of these five was a chaste virgin, Mary, a descendant of the chosen race of whom Christ was directly born (Matt. 1:16). The other women, Tamar, Rahab, Ruth, and Bathsheba, the wife of Uriah, were Gentiles, and some were extremely sinful. This indicates that Christ is related not only to the Jews but also to the Gentiles, and is the kingly Savior of typical sinners. Such a revelation from the first chapter of

Matthew comes from knowing the word as knowledge along with the exercising of prayer. We need to ask the Lord why there are five women in the genealogy of Christ in Matthew 1. As we study who these women are and what they did in a spirit of prayer, we can receive the Lord's revelation.

This genealogy also tells us that Jacob begot Judah and his brothers (1:2), but it does not say that Isaac begot Jacob and his brother. In the Lord's light we can see that Jacob's brother was not chosen by God, so Christ had nothing to do with him. But all the brothers of Judah were chosen by God to compose the twelve tribes of Israel, and they all were related to Christ. As we exercise our spirit to pray over the word and dive into the word with a spirit of prayer, the Lord's light will illumine us with divine revelation.

There is even divine revelation in the name Methuselah (Gen. 5:22). When Enoch had lived sixty-five years, he begot a son and gave him this name. The name Methuselah has a prophetic significance. It means "when he is dead, it shall be sent." By naming his son Methuselah, Enoch prophesied of the coming judgment of the deluge, the great flood at the time of Noah. Nine hundred sixty-nine years later, the age at which Methuselah died, the deluge at Noah's time came (see *Life-study of Genesis*, pp. 357-359). In the name of Methuselah there is a revelation of God. This revelation comes from turning our mind to our spirit when we get into the word. When we come to the Bible, we should not exercise our mind too much. Rather, we have to restrict our mind and turn our mind to our spirit by praying with what we understand from the word. Then the word of wisdom will come to us, and this word of wisdom is the revelation.

In the book of Ephesians there are many words of wisdom, but for us to obtain these words we need to exercise our spirit to pray over this book. The proper revelation comes from our understanding through the prayer connected to our spirit. When we pray much by staying in the presence of the Lord, we will get a clear word from the Lord in our understanding that brings revelation. At times we have to wait on the Lord by stopping our entire being, including our speaking and thinking. Then wisdom will be imparted into us, and that wisdom will become our revelation. I saw the matter of God's New Testament economy with the divine dispensing in the book of Ephesians by staying in the presence of the Lord in quiet prayer over my understanding of the word of knowledge. Then the light came, and that light brought in the wisdom which became the very revelation. I hope that we would learn to pray over the word of God in such a way to get into its depths. Among today's Christians, there is a lack of the word of wisdom and even a lack of the word of knowledge. In many seminaries, they may study the language, history, and archeology of the Bible. But who graduates from a seminary with a rich deposit of the word of knowledge and of the word of wisdom?

By the Lord's mercy, the word spoken in the Lord's recovery is either the word of knowledge or the word of wisdom. As we establish meetings in the homes of the new believers, we need to bring them into the printed ministry that is full of the word of knowledge and the word of wisdom. Every educated person likes to read something, so after the new ones get saved and baptized, we need to furnish them with some reading material. The word in the Lord's recovery will supply them with life, light, truth, and Spirit. The books that we have published, especially *God's New Testament Economy,* are full of words of wisdom. The table of contents of our hymnal, including the arrangement of the topics for the hymns, needed a great deal of wisdom to compose. By studying the hymnal with an exercised spirit, we can receive revelation concerning the proper theology.

In the Lord's recovery there is no lack of the word, but we have to spend time to get into the word by spending time to wait on the Lord. How much time we spend to wait on Him determines how much revelation we will receive. If we spend the proper time in the Lord's presence with the word, we will be persons filled with the word and soaked in the word to be one with the word. Then whenever we go to the home meetings, we will be living factors. We must learn how to use the *Life Lessons,* the *Truth Lessons,* and the Life-study Messages. We have to learn how to handle the word to help people receive God's word in the best way of understanding so that everyone in the home meetings can be nourished, enlightened, and strengthened. The only thing that can build up, nourish, strengthen, and empower the new believers is the divine word. They need the constant word, the instant word, the word of wisdom, and the word of knowledge. We must be able to minister the divine word to the new ones and to all the saints. Then spontaneously all the meetings in the homes will be built up, and a strong church life will be seen in all the home meetings.

I hope all of us would learn to dive into the word according to the fellowship we have received in this chapter. We need to spend time every day in the word. This does not necessarily mean that we need to drop our jobs to serve the Lord with all of our time. Many of us need to work to make a living to support our family and to take care of our children's education. But, generally speaking, in America people only have to work eight hours a day and five days a week. As long as we can make a sufficient living to support our family and take care of our children's education, we should be satisfied. Then we must endeavor to spend the rest of our time to go out to visit others by knocking on their doors and by establishing home meetings in all the new homes. To do this divine work we need to be completed. The Lord Jesus as the Christ of God was completed. Now we, as the ambassadors and ministers of the New Testament, need to be completed, equipped, with the mingled spirit and with the all-inclusive word in many aspects. Through this equipping, we will be qualified and very effective in helping the home meetings.

Chapter Nine

THE BASIC FACTORS FOR THE CHRISTIAN MEETINGS

(3)

Scripture Reading: 1 Thes. 5:17; Acts 4:31; Eph. 6:18; 1 Cor. 14:15; Col. 3:16; Eph. 5:19

As we have seen, the first two factors for the Christian meetings are the mingled spirit and the word. In this chapter we want to see two more factors: praying and singing. The home meetings need much prayer and much singing. If we are really filled and saturated with the Spirit and the word, we will be persons praying unceasingly and singing all the time. Praying and singing come out of our being filled with the Spirit and saturated with the word. We must be men of the Spirit and of the word. Then spontaneously we will be praying and singing persons. These four factors are present in our experience to some extent, but that extent is not so high. We take care of the Spirit, but not that much. We learn the word, but not as much as we should. We may pray every day, but we do not pray unceasingly. We may sing and praise, but we do not sing and praise all the time.

Our daily living needs to be saturated with the Spirit, the word, prayer, and singing so that we can be strong, living, new, and fresh to take care of the home meetings. The home meetings always need people who are fresh, living, excited, and even exciting. We need to be an exciting factor in the meetings to make the others excited. Only the four factors of the mingled spirit, the word, praying, and singing can constitute us into such a person. We need to fan into flame the gift of God which is in us (2 Tim. 1:6).

PRAYING

We must learn to pray all the time. We need to call on

the name of the Lord throughout the day and talk to the Lord. We can talk to the Lord by using short sentences as part of our unceasing prayer. We can pray, "O Lord Jesus, be with me," or "O Lord Jesus, help me." At least we need to keep a praying spirit all the time. During every occupation we can pray, and we have to pray. This prayer will make us men of God. Prayer is the very means through which we contact God.

God created us in a marvelous way. He created us with two ears for us to listen. He created us with two eyes for us to see. We need to eat, so God created us with a mouth. We need to speak, so God created us with a tongue and with vocal cords. We need to digest our food, so God created us with a stomach. We need to breathe, so God created us with lungs. God created everything with a purpose. He created us with a spirit for us to pray. Even unbelievers will pray at certain times, especially when they are in distress or trouble. The Chinese may say, "O heaven help me!" This is their prayer. The Lord Jesus used heaven as a symbol of the highest authority, the almighty God (Luke 15:18). At certain times, unbelievers will pray, "O God, help me!" We do have a praying organ within us, and we do have a praying intent, a praying desire within us. Many of us can testify that the most enjoyable time is the time of prayer.

We fallen human beings like to talk more than pray. We may say that we do not have time to pray, but we may have much time to talk on the telephone. To some people, the telephone is like sticky fly paper. When some people touch the phone, they get stuck to it. Many Americans cannot live without the telephone. The telephone is like breathing to them. They may not have time to do anything, but they always have time to talk on the phone. Too much talk on the telephone will kill your prayer life. When we come together with some saints, it is better to pray and reduce our talk. We all like to talk, but we need to turn our talk to prayer. Too much talk kills, but praying enlivens. When we pray for only five minutes, we get enlivened and we become powerful.

Whenever I go to speak, I must prepare myself by

prayer. The secret of giving a proper message is the first sentence of that message. If the first sentence is uttered properly, the entire message will be right. The way to have the first sentence uttered properly is by the preparation of prayer. I must pray before the message. Likewise, when we go to the homes, we must pray first. Many of the saints who have gone out to visit people by knocking on their doors can testify concerning the power of prayer. Sometimes during their visiting, the doors would not open to them, so they stopped to pray. After their prayer, the first door opened to them and the ones there were baptized. Prayer can maneuver, direct, and control the environment. We have to be praying persons.

We need to be those who pray before the meeting. To pray before the meeting we must be a praying person who prays unceasingly (1 Thes. 5:17). We need to pray unceasingly by calling on the name of the Lord. According to Acts 4:31, we also need to pray in the meeting: "And as they were beseeching, the place in which they were gathered was shaken, and they were all filled with the Holy Spirit, and spoke the word of God with boldness." In the meetings it is good to call on the Lord's name, pray-read the Word, and pray the verses of the hymns. But we also need longer prayers and shorter prayers in our meetings. We need all kinds of divine, living expressions. We need singing, shouting, repeating, calling, and proper long or short prayers.

To pray at the beginning and at the end of the meeting may stir up, strengthen, and enrich the meeting. The more prayer there is in the meeting, the better. We may pray at the beginning and at the end of the meeting, but we should not make this something legal or formal. During the meeting, proper prayer may also render help to the meeting. We do not pray during the meeting often, but a proper prayer during the meeting may be very helpful. When we pray in this way, we should have the assurance that our flesh is not involved. In public prayer, it is possible for us to make a show in our flesh (Matt. 6:5-6). This has to be condemned. We must be fully in the spirit in a pure motive without any intention to express or glorify ourself. Our prayer in the meeting should not be formal nor should it always be by certain persons. In certain localities, I saw that only one or two brothers would pray. In every meeting, all the saints knew that these two would pray. We have to charge the saints to pray and lead them into prayer in the meeting.

We should always pray by exercising the spirit (Eph. 6:18; 1 Cor. 14:15a). Exercising the spirit means not waiting for the Spirit's inspiration but taking the initiative by pushing our spirit to pray. Whenever we pray, we should turn to our spirit, exercising the depths of our being.

SINGING

Our home meetings should be filled with singing. Singing comes out of being filled with grace (Col. 3:16c). When we have an inner realization of God's grace, this realization will stir up our being to sing. Singing also comes out of being filled with the word (Col. 3:16a). When we are filled with the word, the Spirit bubbles from within us in lauding melodies. When the word of Christ fills us up from within, we will spontaneously flow out in singing. Our singing will be in psalms, hymns, and spiritual songs. Psalms are long poems, hymns are shorter ones, and spiritual songs are the shortest. We also need to sing by exercising the spirit (1 Cor. 14:15b). We should not merely sing in our happiness. We should sing joyfully in our spirit. Our singing must come out from our spirit. In praying, in singing, in reading the word, and in touching the Spirit, the secret is to exercise our spirit.

Many saints come to the meeting, yet they do not exercise their spirit. Thus, it is hard to tell if they have a regenerated spirit. I was once with Brother Nee when some co-workers asked him why a certain brother never exercised his spirit although he had been with us for over thirty years. When Brother Nee responded to this question, he jokingly said, "This person might be saved, but not regenerated." Brother Nee meant that this person belonged to the Lord, but it seemed that he was not regenerated because his spirit still remained in a deadened situation. In the church meetings, I have noticed that many persons like to be gentlemen. They think that when they exercise their spirit, they will be crazy men. They do not like to be crazy, but instead they like to be proper gentlemen. Others may shout, call on the name of the Lord, and sing in the meetings, but these ones never exercise their spirit. If all the attendants in our meeting were like this, that meeting would be a graveyard, a cemetery. Years ago I told the saints that the most quiet and calm place is Forest Lawn Cemetery in Los Angeles. Sometimes the Christian meetings are like a cemetery.

To prevent our meetings from being dead, we must learn to pick up the four basic factors for our Christian meetings. We should be mingled with the Spirit, soaked and saturated with the living word, and we should be praying and singing. Then we will be equipped, qualified, and completed to be the proper visitors to knock on people's doors and set up home meetings. We will be a good example to the new ones in their home meetings. The children always like to follow, to copy, to learn, of their parents. When we go to the meetings, we must be a living person and a living example of one who loves the word, who is always filled with the Spirit, and who is singing and praying. Then our presence will be a great help and a great factor to strengthen and enrich the meeting.

LIVING ACCORDING TO GOD'S ORDAINED WAY TO PRACTICE HIS NEW TESTAMENT ECONOMY

As people who love the Lord, we must live according to God's ordained way to practice His New Testament economy. We need to take care of our living, and then spend the rest of our time to visit people by knocking on their doors in prayer in order to get them baptized and to set up home meetings. Two saints bringing in twelve new ones a year would result in an increase of twenty-four. Twenty-four new ones can compose a proper local church. Every year a new church could be produced by our taking the Lord's new way. After we go out to visit others and baptize them, we must endeavor to take care of them through the home meetings. We need to be like the nursing mothers who cherish their own children (1 Thes. 2:7). If the churches are faithful to the Lord's new way, many new churches can be raised up within a short amount of time. We who go to take care of the home meetings to establish them and build them into local churches must be persons filled with the Spirit, soaked in the word, praying unceasingly, and singing all the time. Then we will be happy in the Lord, crazy with the enjoyment of Christ, and the doors of the homes that we visit will open to us.

If some doors will not open to us, we need to go and visit them again. In Taipei some homes were visited four or five times. When the saints visited one home for the fifth time, the host of this house told them that he admired their endurance and that he was ready to be baptized. A number of genuine believers were produced by our going to them again and again with longsuffering. When we go to visit others in a proper way, the Holy Spirit goes out with us. He goes in our going because He has been waiting for us to go for years. In the book of Isaiah the Lord exclaimed, "Whom shall I send, and who will go for us" (6:8). We all need to respond in the same way that Isaiah did: "Here am I; send me" (v. 8).

We do not invite people to the gospel, but we bring the gospel to people. To visit others is to follow God's pattern. When Adam fell, God immediately came to visit him, and asked Adam, "Where are you?" (Gen. 3:9). God was not sitting on the throne asking Adam to come to Him. God did not invite Adam to come to Him to hear the gospel. Instead, God brought the gospel to Adam. Eventually, God became a man to come down to the earth to visit people. He came down from heaven to save sinners (1 Tim. 1:15), He visited Zaccheus (Luke 19:1-10), He visited the Samaritan woman (John 4:3-42), He sent the twelve disciples to visit people (Matt. 10:5-8, 11-13), and He sent the seventy to visit people (Luke 10:1-6). He told the seventy that He was sending them as lambs in the midst of wolves (v. 3), but in the midst of these wolves were sons of peace (v. 6). By our visiting people, we will discover who the sons of peace are. Then these sons of peace will be regenerated and eventually transformed. They will be the members of Christ to form His Body in order to accomplish God's eternal economy. Christianity has missed God's ordained way. In Christendom, big halls, cathedrals, and chapels are built to invite people to come to hear the gospel. But today the Lord has shown us that all the members of the church should be visitors going out to bring the gospel to people. We have to go to visit people and send meetings to their homes. If we ask people to come to our meeting hall, the majority will not come. But we can take our meetings to the homes. We can carry out the burden to provide these homes with "food to go." We do not need to ask them to come to buy our food and eat our food. We need to send food to their homes.

In the Lord's new way, we must do these two things: go to visit people and go to establish and care for home meetings. If we are going to do this, we must be persons one with the mingling Spirit, soaked in the living word, praying unceasingly, and singing all the time. We have published a four volume series entitled *Life Lessons* for the nourishment of the new believers in their homes. At the end of each lesson there is a hymn. We need to sing these hymns and songs in the home meetings to stir up the spirits of the attendants. We should practice singing all the time (Eph. 5:19). Singing encourages people and makes them fresh and living. Today on this earth there are many burdens and much discouragement. When we go to the homes of the new believers in the evening, our singing of the songs in the *Life Lessons* will stir them up and encourage them. We must learn to be praying persons and singing persons. If we are such persons, our home meetings will be very fresh, new, living, and enlivening.

CHAPTER TEN

GOD'S ORDAINED WAY TO SPREAD THE GOSPEL

Scripture Reading: Gen. 3:8-9, 15, 21; Exo. 3:8; 1 Tim. 1:15; Luke 19:1-10; John 4:3-15; Matt. 10:5-8, 11-13; Luke 10:1-6; Mark 16:15; Matt. 28:19

GOD'S PATTERN

In the Bible there is a way ordained by God to spread the gospel. God's pattern of spreading the gospel is seen in Genesis and Exodus.

Genesis records the first time in the entire universe that God Himself directly visited fallen man. First God came to find fallen man, then God preached the gospel to fallen man, and finally God ministered salvation to the condemned man. In Genesis at Adam's fall, God came to find him (3:8-9). God was the first "door-knocker." He came to "knock on Adam's door" immediately after Adam sinned by eating the fruit of the tree of the knowledge of good and evil. Although Adam hid himself from the presence of God, God came to find him. He came to visit Adam, to knock on the door of Adam's heart. He called unto Adam and said to him, "Where are you?" (v. 9). After God found fallen man, He preached the gospel to him (Gen. 3:15). God told fallen man that the seed of the woman would bruise the head of the damaging serpent. The seed of the woman was Jesus Christ who was born of a virgin, and He bruised the head of the old serpent, the Devil, on the cross.

Furthermore, God ministered salvation to the condemned man (Gen. 3:21). God made coats of skins to cover fallen man, and those skins came from a slain sacrifice. The coats of skins signify Christ as the very righteousness from God to cover us. Before being covered by these coats of skins, Adam and Eve were afraid to be seen by God so they clothed themselves with fig leaves sown together (3:7).

But God came in to clothe them in a proper way, signifying that God's salvation clothes fallen man with Christ Himself. God's clothing of fallen man was a type of God's covering salvation.

God's pattern of visiting man can also be seen at the time of Israel's fall. Israel had fallen deeply into Egyptian bondage. Then God came down to visit them. In Exodus 3:8 the Lord said, "I am come down to deliver them out of the hand of the Egyptians." God came down to visit Israel in order to deliver them out of the usurping hand and the tyranny of Pharaoh in Egypt.

THE LORD'S EXAMPLE

The New Testament reveals the example of the Lord Jesus Christ in visiting man. He came down from heaven to save sinners (1 Tim. 1:15). For Him to come down means that He went out to visit the sinful race. We all have to follow the Lord Jesus as our pattern to go out to visit fallen human beings. Furthermore, the Lord went to visit Zaccheus with His dynamic salvation (Luke 19:1-10). The Lord told Zaccheus, "Today I must stay in your house" (v. 5), and "Today salvation has come to this house" (v. 9). The Lord's word shows us that the unit of God's salvation is not an individual person, but the whole family, the whole house.

The Lord also set an example in going to visit the Samaritan woman to bring her the living water (John 4:3-15). John 4:4 tells us that the Lord Jesus "had to pass through Samaria." The Lord had left Judea and was on His way to Galilee. The Lord had to pass through Samaria because He had to go to Jacob's well to wait for that sinful, Samaritan woman. He went to the well to bring her the real living water of salvation. This story of salvation took place not in a chapel or a cathedral but in the open air near Jacob's well. We should follow this pattern of the Lord Jesus in going to visit sinners for their salvation.

THE LORD'S SENDING THE DISCIPLES

Also in the Gospels, we can see the Lord sending the

disciples. He sent the twelve to go to the cities and villages to visit the lost sheep of the house of Israel and bring them peace (Matt. 10:5-8, 11-13). While the Lord Jesus was physically on this earth, He did not practice calling meetings, but He always went to visit. He visited Galilee, Judea, and Jerusalem. He visited Martha and Mary's home (Luke 10:38-39) and the house of Simon the leper (Matt. 26:6). The Lord carried out His ministry all the time by visiting people. The practice of visiting people to bring them the salvation and riches of the Triune God is absolutely in contrast with the practice of today's deformed and degraded Christianity. We must be rescued from that kind of degraded situation back to the Lord's way.

When the Lord sent the twelve, He charged them to go to cities and villages to visit the lost sheep. We should follow the Lord to do the same thing by going to new cities and small towns. The number twelve bears a particular significance in the Scriptures. Twelve is composed of four times three, the Triune God (three) multiplied by man (four). Twelve refers to the mingling of the Triune God with the tripartite man. If we have gospel groups composed of twelve saints, there can be four teams with three saints on each team. We are linked up with the Triune God going out to knock on people's doors. We go out as people who are mingled with the Triune God.

The Lord also sent the seventy to go to every city and place to seek the sons of peace (Luke 10:1-6), and we have to do likewise. According to Luke 10 these sons of peace are in the midst of wolves (v. 3). A person may be a son of rebellion one evening and a son of peace the next. A husband may have had an argument with his wife, and when you go to visit him, he may be a son of rebellion that evening. But the next day something might happen to make him happy. When you go to him that evening, he may be a son of peace. That may be the right time for you to sow the seed of the divine life into his being. We should not be disappointed with being rejected when we go out to visit people by knocking on their doors. Before we were saved, we also were sons of rebellion, but one day we became sons of peace. God prepared all of us to receive the gospel. At one time we were rebellious toward God, but one day we changed our attitude. At the right time the gospel came to us, and we repented, believed in the Lord Jesus, and were saved. If we have the patience and endurance to knock on the same door again and again, the ones who live there may eventually become sons of peace. We need to follow the Lord Jesus' example to go visit every city and every place to seek the sons of peace.

The Lord Jesus sent all His disciples to go into all the world and preach the gospel to all the creation (Mark 16:15). They were charged to disciple all the nations by baptizing them into the Triune God (Matt. 28:19). All the creation needs to hear the gospel. If we do not have men to preach to, we can preach to the flowers and to the animals. This will increase our faith and cultivate our utterance. Some people have told me that they do not know what to say when they speak to others. My advice to them is to speak to the creation, which includes all the creatures. If we do this, we will learn how to speak. The gospel should be preached to all the creation. If we are crazy with the enjoyment of Christ, we will talk to everything we see about the gospel. If we are speaking the gospel all the time, we will eventually be prevailing, and our preaching will be full of power. Soon after I received the Lord, I practiced speaking by the seashore to the ocean. I did not learn how to preach in a seminary but at the seashore by talking to the sea.

GOING OUT TO VISIT PEOPLE
BEING THE MOST EFFECTIVE WAY
TO SPREAD THE GOSPEL FOR THE KINGDOM OF GOD

Going out to visit people is the most effective way to spread the gospel for the kingdom of God. Actually, visiting people by knocking on their doors is not a new way but an ancient way. This way began from the garden in Genesis 3. Every Christian should knock on people's doors to bring others the gospel. To knock on people's doors means to visit people. To visit people by knocking on their doors is actually the God-ordained, Christian way to spread the gospel that has been picked up by the Mormons and Jehovah's Witnesses to spread their heretical teaching. It is regrettable that the proper people, the Christians, have nearly given up the God-ordained way to spread the gospel. But now the Lord is leading us back to this way.

We have to take the way of going out to visit people by learning how to do it and by being trained. The greatest hindrance to our being trained to go out to visit people is our concept. We may be holding on to our past practice of preaching the gospel. Our past practice may have been good, but it is not nearly as effective as our present practice of going out to visit people. The first requirement of our being trained in the new way is to drop our concept. We must drop our concepts and pick up the instructions of the training. We cannot be trained by the Lord if we hold on to our old practice. If we would forget about our old way and pick up the Lord's new way, we will see the positive results.

In the Lord's new way we must be believing, assured, bold, and aggressive. We have been sent to visit people by the ascended Christ, and while we are talking to people we are linked to Christ. We have the position and the authority of the ascended Christ to direct people to believe and be baptized. Because we have been entrusted with the authority of the ascended Christ to preach the gospel, we should not ask people questions. We should not ask, "Will you believe?" We need to direct them to believe. We should not ask others if they want to be baptized, but we need to direct them to be baptized. We need to be like John the Baptist who told people, "Repent, for the kingdom of the heavens has drawn near" (Matt. 3:2). John the Baptist preached with an imperative, not with questions.

In our natural man we always want to be nice, good, and humble. We like to ask others, "Would you please believe in the Lord Jesus?" But if we ask others questions in this way, we will be rejected most of the time. Our asking of questions opens the door for rejection. We need to speak everything in the way of a command. We are the

Lord's heavenly ambassadors who have been committed with all the authority in heaven and on earth to baptize people into the Triune God. We need to direct people to repent and confess their sins. We need to lead them to pray. After a little prayer we need to tell them that they are now ready to be baptized. If we would exercise this divine authority, many of the people we visit will be like lambs. We will be able to lead them out of the kingdom of Satan into the kingdom of God. The most effective way to preach the gospel is not to ask questions but to direct people to repent, pray, and be baptized. When we baptize a person into the Triune God, he will become another person. Baptism changes people because we are baptizing them into the name of the Triune God, which is the sum total of the divine Being.

To go out to visit people for the spread of the gospel by knocking on their doors is altogether reasonable and logical. The gospel should be spread and preached, and the best way to bring the gospel to others is to go to them by knocking on their doors. All of us should take the initiative, and be bold to practice this. We do not need to get agreement from the church to visit people to spread the gospel. For the leading ones in a locality to require the saints to come to them in order to get their agreement to go out to knock on doors is wrong. We do not have to get the church to agree with us in order to breathe or to eat. In like manner, as branches of the vine we have to bear fruit, and we do not need to get anyone's agreement to do this. We must bear fruit if we are to remain in the vine, so we all have to exercise our boldness to go out to visit people to spread the gospel for the kingdom of God.

CHAPTER ELEVEN

THE DESTINY OF THE BRANCHES OF THE DIVINE TRINITY'S ORGANISM

Scripture Reading: John 15:1-8, 16; Acts 2:46; 5:42

THE DIVINE TRINITY'S ORGANISM

God is triune and in His Godhead, in His divine person, there is the divine Trinity. This divine Trinity needs an organic entity, an organism, to bear fruit for His expression. The divine Trinity's organism is the universal true vine and the branches (John 15:1-5). The vine is the embodiment of the entire divine Trinity, the Father, the Son, and the Spirit. The branches are the enlargement of the vine. The universal true vine and its branches as revealed in John 15 should be considered as a reality more than as a metaphor. The organism of the divine Trinity in John 15 is the divine Trinity mingled with His chosen, redeemed, and regenerated people. The greatest fact in the entire universe is that God in His divine Trinity mingled Himself with us to constitute us into an organism to carry out His intention, to bear His expression for His glory.

In England in 1958 a friend took me to see the Queen's vine, a very large vine enclosed in a greenhouse. My friend exclaimed to me, "How great is this vine!" But I responded that the Queen's vine was very small compared to Christ as the true vine, who is so great that He fills the entire universe. Christ as the vine is tremendously long. This vine reaches every place on the globe by its branches.

THE DESTINY OF THE BRANCHES—TO BEAR FRUIT

Our destiny as branches of the universal true vine is to bear fruit (John 15:2-5) for the glorification, the expression, of the Father (v. 8). The danger of not bearing fruit is to be cut off, dried up, and burned (vv. 2, 6). To be cut off from the vine is to lose all the life supply and nourishment of the vine. Many Christians consider that bearing fruit depends upon the environment and that not bearing fruit is therefore excusable. Fruit-bearing, however, is not a matter of our environment; it is our destiny. We have been destined by God to bear fruit. Because many Christians have not borne any fruit for many years, God's destiny has been annulled in them. The best way to carry out God's destiny of bearing fruit is to visit people by knocking on their doors. Visiting people by knocking on their doors has been fully proven by experience as the best way to bear fruit.

You do not need the agreement from your church before you can knock on doors to bear fruit. To bear fruit is your destiny. The leading ones should not say, "You must wait before going out to knock on doors until we get everything prepared for the whole church." This is unreasonable. Bearing fruit is like breathing. To ask someone to wait until something is prepared before bearing fruit is like asking someone to stop breathing. We must not wait to bear fruit. We should go out to knock on doors and bear remaining fruit by setting up home meetings. Such fruit will convince others that visiting people is the way to bear fruit.

In the past when the saints brought a person to the Lord, our practice was to get the church's approval before he could be baptized. But the new ones who believe should be baptized immediately. No permission is needed from the church to baptize them. Around 1930, in Shanghai there was a young man who received the Lord and was planning to study in the United States. Brother Nee was very burdened that this young man be baptized immediately before he left China, but one of the leading ones would not agree. He felt that since this new brother had only recently heard the gospel and believed, it would be risky to baptize him and that without testing, no one knew whether his belief was genuine or not. Brother Nee replied that he would bear the responsibility for the new brother's baptism, but the elder still insisted that baptism should be through the church's approval. Eventually Brother Nee relented,

THE DESTINY OF THE BRANCHES

yet he never agreed with this kind of practice regarding baptism.

God has chosen us and sent us to bear fruit. God's destiny for us is to bear fruit, so we must go out to knock on doors, visit people, help them to believe, and baptize them. Our statistics show that out of twenty doors that we knock on, one person will be baptized. We must redeem the time to knock on more doors in order to find the sons of peace (Luke 10:6).

THE NEW WAY VERSUS THE TRADITIONAL WAY

According to some recent statistics collected in England, all the major denominations in that country, such as the Catholic Church and the Church of England, have decreased in numbers by twenty-five percent since 1970. Only one group, the Home Church, which began after 1970, has increased. In the United States, many of the big denominations have also decreased. Among those who have increased, the highest rate of increase has been about six percent each year. The reason for this decrease and slight increase in numbers among the denominations is that the traditional way, a degradation from the God-ordained way, does not work well.

During the fifteen years prior to October 1984, we were influenced by the traditional way. Yet when the ministry began in Taiwan in 1949, we increased from about five hundred on the entire island to about fifty thousand in the first five or six years. In those years, there was a hundredfold increase mainly through the practice of meeting in the small groups. After 1960, however, when I left Taiwan to come to the United States, the number of saints gradually decreased, and the small group practice was nearly annulled.

When I went back to Taipei in 1984, the practice was nearly the same as the denominations. Big meetings were held with good, eloquent speakers appointed to speak good messages. Everyone appreciated this kind of meeting. However, I reminded them that the church in Taipei had over twenty-two thousand members in 1959. In 1984, approximately twenty-five years later, the church in Taipei had only eleven thousand members. There had been good meetings, good speakers, and good messages, yet the number of people had been reduced. Pointing out this situation to the saints, I said, "We have been on this small island for twenty-five years with forty thousand believers under our edification, yet the island has not been evangelized. What is the good of preaching the principle of Christ's death and resurrection and of having good meetings? Regardless of how good the present way seems, it does not work well. Saints, you must change your way!" In Taiwan I have the complete ground and God-given position to tell the saints to change their way because the Lord used me to begin and establish the work there.

In 1950 Brother Nee brought a revival to Hong Kong, and he asked me to go there to arrange all the services of the co-workers, elders, and deacons. In 1954 I returned to Hong Kong to minister the word, and the hall was crowded with over one thousand people. Since that time, however, there has been very little increase in Hong Kong. The low rate of increase in the churches is a shame to us.

The work among us in the United States has also been increasing very slowly over the past ten years. From the beginning of the Lord's move in the United States in the early sixties, our rate of increase was between twenty to thirty percent each year. But in the last ten years the rate of increase, especially in Orange County, has only been about three percent each year. In all of the churches throughout the United States, the low rate of increase concerned me very much.

When I finished writing the notes for the Recovery Version of the New Testament to complete a twelve year Life-study of the New Testament, I realized that it was the time for me to go back to Taiwan to have a new start. I could no longer tolerate the situation among the churches of very little increase. I began to study Christian history and our own history of sixty years. I reconsidered what

THE DESTINY OF THE BRANCHES

was mentioned in the Bible concerning the way of Christian meeting. The Lord brought me to see that the traditional way of Christianity was absolutely wrong and was an annulling and killing way. Therefore, I made a strong decision to change our method, our way. I likened the change of our way to the change in transportation on the globe. The globe can never be changed, but the transportation on the globe changes and improves all the time. In the 1930s I traveled by boat from Chefoo to Shanghai in mainland China, and the trip took about forty-eight hours. During those trips, I got seasick. Today I can fly on a jet plane all the way from Los Angeles to Taipei in only about twelve hours. During such a trip, I can sleep and eat well. Thank God for the improvement of transportation. Man's mode of transportation has evolved and improved from the mule wagon to the jetliner. Likewise, the Bible can never be changed, but our way must be changed and improved. We cannot change the Bible, the Lord Jesus, God, the truth, the gospel, salvation, or any of the divine things, yet we can surely change our way!

I made the decision to come back to the biblical way, that is, the God-ordained way to preach the gospel in the homes, to set up meetings in the homes, to edify the saints in the homes, and to build up the church in the homes. Home sweet home! In this new way there are just two words: Go! Home! We should go out of our own homes and bring the Bible, the gospel, the Lord Jesus, the Triune God, grace, light, life, and the dynamic salvation into the new ones' homes! Do not ask them to come to us; rather, we must go to them to set up the church meeting in their homes. We will fulfill our destiny to bear fruit by going out to others' homes.

It is unreasonable and illogical to doubt that this new way will work. What way is more effective than this way? Many of the saints over the past several years have not baptized anyone, yet in a few days of going out to visit people by knocking on their doors, they have baptized five, six, or seven in one evening! Even to baptize one makes this way worthwhile. The God-ordained way fulfills our God-made destiny as branches to bear fruit.

THE PURPOSE OF THE LORD'S CHOOSING

The purpose of the Lord's choosing, His appointment of us, is to bear fruit (John 15:16). Fruit-bearing is not only God's destiny assigned to us, but it is also God's appointment to us. God destined us and appointed us to bear fruit, but many of us had no feeling about being barren in the past. One leading one had not baptized anyone as fruit for twenty years, yet he had little feeling about it. Since returning from a trip to Taipei, however, he has baptized about one each week. What a difference! For a branch to bear fruit is crucial; otherwise, it will lose all of the enjoyment, riches, nourishment, and life supply of the vine.

THE WAY TO BEAR FRUIT
AND TO HAVE THE FRUIT REMAIN

The way to bear fruit is by abiding in the vine (John 15:4-5), by being supplied with the Lord's instant words (v. 7), and by going forth (v. 16a). The living, instant words of the Lord always come when we bear fruit. We bear fruit by going forth. Some Bible teachers have said that the fruit in John 15 is the fruit of our character, such as good ethics, good morality, and good virtues. I would not say that this is wrong, but the word "go forth" in John 15:16 indicates that the fruit is living persons. The Lord charged us to go forth and bear fruit. To bear ethical virtues, we do not need to go forth. But to bear fruit among people, we need to go forth to people's homes. To bear fruit is the way to fulfill God's destiny, and the way to bear fruit is to visit people by knocking on their doors. The way to have fruit that remains (v. 16b) is by setting up home meetings with the new believers (Acts 2:46; 5:42) and by praying for the home meetings of the believers.

THE MULTIPLICATION AND SPREAD OF THE
PROCESSED TRIUNE GOD

The divine Trinity's organism is for the multiplication and spread of the processed Triune God. This organism is to have the processed Triune God multiplied in millions of His chosen ones.

CHAPTER TWELVE

SETTING UP HOME MEETINGS

Scripture Reading: Acts 2:46; 5:42; 1 Cor. 14:26; Rom. 12:4-5; Eph. 4:16; 1 Cor. 12:1-3, 8; 14:6

In the Lord's new way to carry out the increase and spread of the church, we have discovered that setting up home meetings is more difficult than going out to knock on doors and baptize people. We must endeavor to learn how to raise up home meetings. We must pray for a living way to bring the new believers onward that they may grow in life, in knowledge, and in function as members of the Lord's Body. I would encourage you to read the following books on the home meetings which have been recently published by Living Stream Ministry: *Key Points on the Home Meetings; The Home Meetings—The Unique Way for the Increase and the Building Up of the Church; The Living Needed for Building Up the Small Group Meetings;* and *On Home Meetings.*

FORSAKING CHRISTIANITY'S TRADITIONAL WAY OF MEETING

A piano student must follow his teacher's instructions to play in the trained way. Likewise, we must practice the New Testament economy in the trained way and not in a way according to our natural disposition. Apparently, it is easy to visit people by knocking on their doors, but in recent years we have found that there is a science to knocking on doors. The Lord's new way is effective, but it only works in the trained, disciplined way, not in the natural way. Once we take the natural way, knocking on doors becomes ineffectual.

We need more training to set up home meetings. We may consider that coming together to meet is easy and can be done in a natural way. Anyone can gather a group of people to have a meeting in a natural or religious way, but to have a proper Christian meeting according to God's ordained way is not easy. The religious way always teaches people to give reverence to God and to worship Him. Christians and unbelievers can come together to worship God according to their natural thought in a natural and religious way. Many in Christendom are nominal Christians who have many concepts concerning how to worship God. First, they may consider that in gathering to worship God there is the need of a chapel or a cathedral. Then after coming into the place of worship, they would look for the leader. According to Christianity's traditional way of meeting there must also be a choir. Without the priest or pastor and a choir, some might consider that this is not the proper place to come to worship God. In a traditional service there is usually the formal reading of the Bible, and after the service the attendants wait for a blessing or benediction from the pastor. Without these traditional, religious, and formal things, many would not consider their meeting to be the proper worship of God. The background of our culture, family, and history can have an influence on the way we meet. We must forget about the natural, religious way of meeting according to the traditional way of Christianity. Singing is effective for the new way, but even singing could be made religious if we sing apart from Christ.

In preaching the gospel, teaching the truth, leading people to worship God, and setting up meetings, what is most crucial is that these things be done in the spirit. In John 4:24 the Lord Jesus told the Samaritan woman, "God is Spirit; and those who worship Him must worship in spirit...." God's substance is Spirit, and we must worship Him in spirit, that is, in our spirit which has been touched, inspired, regenerated, and indwelt by the Spirit of God. Worshipping God is altogether a matter of the divine Spirit and the human spirit. God is the divine Spirit and He created us with a human spirit for us to contact Him as the Spirit.

Some of the fundamental denominations in Christianity

do not like to talk about the Spirit. Many preachers do not preach anything concerning the Spirit because to them the Spirit is too abstract. They do not help people to do anything in the Spirit, so it is very difficult for them to have a proper Christian gathering. At the other extreme, the Pentecostals were raised up in the middle of the preceding century. They stressed the Spirit very much, but they did it in an improper way. In 1932 I attended a meeting with Brother Nee in my home province. Some there were clapping their hands, some were jumping, and others were shouting, crying, and laughing. The pastor was not able to exercise any control in the meeting. After about half an hour, he went to the podium and told the people to stop and be quiet. They did not hear him and continued to shout and clap. After he rang a bell a few times, the noise stopped. Then Brother Nee went to the podium and spoke concerning the loving father and the prodigal son in Luke 15, while the congregation waited for the end of his message. Are we going to set up the home meetings in such a way? We must not set up the home meetings according to the fundamental or the Pentecostal way.

Taiwan is mostly a Buddhist country. When we set up Christian meetings there, the new ones realize that they should not do it according to their background of Buddhism. But in the Western world with the background of Christianity it is quite complicated. Some of this background may be hidden in your heart. If you go out to set up home meetings, what kind of meetings will you set up? Some of you have been with the Pentecostals. Are you going to set up a Pentecostal meeting? Some of you have been with the Brethren. Are you going to set up that kind of meeting?

In 1984 I went back to Taiwan to change the way of meeting. I told the saints that they should not begin the meeting by selecting a hymn or by reading the Bible. I likewise said not to begin the meeting by praying or by giving a message as a pastor. That really bothered the saints. They wondered how they could begin a meeting without any of these things. I even told them not to begin the meeting by calling on the name of the Lord. Perhaps even calling on the Lord might be a religion in the churches. In order to take the new way, we have to drop all the old ways we have picked up and all the things we are accustomed to doing.

The New Testament speaks of many meetings. The Lord Jesus met with the five thousand (John 6:10), and He met with a great crowd on the seashore (Matt. 13:1-2). After His resurrection, He met with His disciples in Galilee (John 20:26-31; 21:1-14). We have published a book entitled *How To Meet,* but the more one reads that book the more he may not know how to meet. Within that book, however, is the New Testament reality of the way to meet. The way to meet is to drop all the natural, religious ways of Christianity by turning to our spirit and living a normal life in the spirit.

Every kind of natural or religious gathering is a performance. The attendants are actors, and their meeting is a "theater." When they come into the meeting, they come as to a theater to act with a mask. A hypocrite, according to Greek, was a stage-actor, one who spoke with a mask. Such were the Pharisees. They were actors; in the meetings they acted in a manner different from their living. The proper Christian meeting, however, should be a living in the meeting that matches our living at home. There should be no performance. We must live properly, speak properly, dress properly, and express ourselves properly. To behave poorly in our daily life but come to the meeting and behave properly is a performance. That is not genuine. Rather, that is a lie and a cheating to people. The traditional meetings of Christianity are "theaters" where people perform.

The way to set up home meetings is first to forsake Christianity's traditional, natural, and religious way of meeting. In the four Gospels the Lord Jesus never set up a schedule of meetings, and He had no meeting hall. In Acts also there were many activities and spontaneous meetings, but there is no record to tell us exactly how they met. Acts only tells us that they preached, taught, broke bread,

SETTING UP HOME MEETINGS

prayed, and had fellowship (Acts 2:42; 5:42). Let us not bring in anything old from Christianity into the new home meetings. We must start to practice the God-ordained way to meet by forsaking the old way.

ANNULLING ORGANIZATION, HIERARCHY, AND THE CLERICAL SYSTEM AND RECOVERING THE GOD-ORDAINED WAY OF MEETING

Furthermore, the way to set up the home meetings is to annul organization, hierarchy, and the clerical system. In our meetings there should not be anyone claiming to have a position over others. We all are nobodies and are all the same in the meeting. No one has any rank. There is no hierarchy, and no one is special or belongs to a special class. In setting up the home meetings we must recover the God-ordained way of meeting from house to house (Acts 2:46; 5:42).

AFFORDING OPPORTUNITIES FOR EACH MEMBER TO FUNCTION IN THE MEETING

We must also afford opportunities for each member to function in the meeting (1 Cor. 14:26). We must set up the home meetings in such a way that every attendant, even a young child, has an equal opportunity to function. Even a young girl can call a hymn or a young boy can start the singing.

PROMOTING AND DEVELOPING THE ORGANIC GIFTS OF EACH MEMBER OF THE BODY OF CHRIST

Then we must learn how to promote and develop, that is, to cultivate, the organic gifts of each member of the Body of Christ (Rom. 12:4-5; Eph. 4:16). All the attendants in the meeting have a gift because they are the members of Christ. Each one's gift comes out of the divine life which he possesses. We have God's life within us, and this life produces something organic. As an infant begins to grow, his organic function begins to be cultivated within him. Eventually he can speak, walk, and do many things. This illustrates the development of the organic gift within us. As regenerated Christians we must let the divine life develop within us, and this development produces the gift of life, the organic gift. However, the practice of Christianity kills the organic function. Christians are encouraged to sit dumbly in the meetings and are not able to function. The way of Christianity is a killing and binding way. Those in this way do not have the adequate opportunity to function.

In the proper Christian meetings we should afford everyone a sufficient time and opportunity to exercise his gifts. Even a young boy of six years of age can say, "Praise the Lord," "Lord Jesus, I love You," or "God is good for food." In every home meeting, we must help all the attendants to develop their organic gifts. This requires that we be a proper pattern, an example, for them to follow. Therefore, we ourselves must forsake the old way and annul anything of organization in the meetings. From the time we first set up a meeting, we must always make it clear that everyone has to function and learn to exercise his spirit. It is remarkable that little children learn language not by being taught but by living among and listening to other speakers. The ability to learn language is born into us. In the same way, every man is born with a human spirit and can call on the name of the Lord. Therefore, we must have the confidence that even the little ones in the meetings can function. In setting up the home meetings we have no intention to organize something to build up a facade to attract people. We must simply help the new ones to meet in their homes to worship God and the Lord Jesus.

MEETING BY THE SPIRIT AND WITH THE WORD AND IMPRESSING THE NEW BELIEVERS WITH THE GOD-ORDAINED WAY

In the home meetings we must also meet by the Spirit (1 Cor. 12:1-3) and with the word of God (1 Cor. 12:8; 14:6). These are the first two basic factors for the Christian meetings. Eventually, we should impress the new believers not with anything of the deformed and degraded Christianity, but with the God-ordained way. We must make a definite and thorough decision not to bring anything of the old way into the home meetings. Once we bring natural and religious things into the meeting, the new ones will be impressed with these things. Then it will be hard to drop them. Be very careful in setting up meetings in the new ones' homes. Simply go there to help them to have a home meeting, and impress them with the God-ordained way to practice the New Testament economy.

CHAPTER THIRTEEN

THE WAY TO BUILD UP HOME MEETINGS

Scripture Reading: Acts 5:42; 2:46, 42; 12:12

CHRISTIAN MEETINGS BEING
FOR THE WORSHIP OF GOD AND THE LORD JESUS

In the home meetings we have to tell the attendants that Christian meetings are for the worship of God and the Lord Jesus. To worship God and the Lord Jesus does not necessarily mean that we have to kneel down or bow down to adore Him with praises and thanks. We can worship God and the Lord Jesus by preaching the gospel, teaching the truth (Acts 5:42), breaking bread to remember the Lord (2:46), fellowshipping one with another (2:42), and praying (2:42; 12:12). In our understanding, in our realization, and in our spirit we should do all things with the sense of worshipping God and the Lord Jesus. We should make this matter clear to all the saints. The New Testament does not indicate to us that to worship God and the Lord Jesus is just a matter of kneeling down or bowing down. The New Testament does tell us, however, that in our Christian meetings we should preach the gospel, teach the truth, break bread to remember the Lord, fellowship one with another, and pray.

To be one with the Lord in preaching the gospel for the salvation of sinners is a kind of worship. When we go out to knock on people's doors to afford the Lord a way to save them, this is counted as a kind of worship to God and the Lord Jesus. John 4 records the Lord Jesus conversing with a sinful Samaritan woman regarding drinking the living water (vv. 10, 14). Eventually the Lord Jesus revealed that to contact God the Spirit with our spirit is to drink of the living water (4:24), and to drink of the living water is to render real worship to God. The sinner was satisfied with the Savior's living water, and the Savior was satisfied with

God's will in satisfying the sinner (4:32). The revelation in John 4 shows us that the worship of God is contrary to the concept of religion.

The Muslims worship God by taking off their shoes and bowing down in prayer for a long period of time. Although this is a mere religious form, they consider that what they are doing is the best worship rendered to God. We Christians do not worship God and the Lord Jesus in that way. One of the ways in which we worship God is by preaching the Lord Jesus as the gospel to save sinners. The Bible does not tell us definitely that when we worship God and the Lord Jesus, we should bow down or kneel down. To think that worshipping God and the Lord Jesus is merely a matter of bowing down or kneeling down is according to the religious concept. We must drop our religious and natural concepts concerning the proper worship of God and the Lord Jesus.

Soon after I received the Lord, I met with a group of Christians who had a prayer meeting every Tuesday night. During that meeting, they always sang a hymn first, and then they knelt down to pray for at least one hour. Quite often while we were kneeling, a number of people fell asleep. I do not think that this constituted a pleasant worship to God. Rather, when we talk one with another in our spirit, the Spirit of God, who is God Himself, participates in our talking. This is the best worship.

Suppose that a loving mother prepared a good dinner for her son who came back home from school after half a year. If this son knelt down and bowed down to the mother and even fell asleep in this posture, do you think the mother would be pleased? She might rebuke her son. The mother will feel happy and pleasant if her son eats the food she has prepared and if he talks to her while he eats. There is a similar record of mutual fellowship in the Old Testament in Genesis 18 between Abraham and God.

Abraham's Worship of God in Genesis 18

Genesis 18 gives us a record of the Lord Jesus coming to Abraham in the form of a man even before His incarnation.

Abraham prepared water for the washing of His physical feet (v. 4), and he asked his wife to prepare a good meal (vv. 6-8). That Man with the two angels ate that dinner, and Abraham served it. We may have never considered that the record in Genesis 18 shows us Abraham's worship to God. Abraham even walked with Jehovah to send Him off, and during this walk, Jehovah talked to Abraham and Abraham prayed (vv. 16-33). Actually, Abraham's prayer was a personal, human, and friendly talk with Jehovah. According to James 2:23 Abraham was called a friend of God. God, as Abraham's friend, opened up His heart to Abraham to tell him of the coming destruction of Sodom and Gomorrah. By this talk, Abraham's divine Friend indicated that Abraham's nephew, Lot, would be damaged. We may say that Abraham's talk to Jehovah was a prayer. Abraham asked Jehovah to do something in order to spare Lot's life and family.

In Genesis 18 there is a record of Abraham's worship, Abraham's prayer, but his worship to God, his prayer, was not in a religious way. His prayer was a personal, human talk. Genesis 18 gives us a record of two friends talking to one another while they walked together. What a beautiful picture of genuine prayer and worship; even in the ancient times in the Old Testament, God came to visit Abraham in a human form and in a human way to receive Abraham's service, Abraham's worship, Abraham's prayer. Abraham's worship, his prayer, was his conversing with God in an intimate, human way as a friend, and this is the best prayer.

I was taught from my youth that the best way to pray was to kneel down. There is nothing wrong with kneeling in prayer, but prayer is not merely a matter of kneeling. The best way to worship, to pray, is to talk to God, to converse with the Lord Jesus in a human way as a part of our daily walk. The picture of the Lord Jesus coming as a friend to Abraham in Genesis 18 is marvelous. The Lord was not sitting on a throne in Genesis 18, telling Abraham, "I am your Master. I am the sovereign One. You have to bow down to Me." The Lord came to Abraham in a human way, visiting Abraham as a friend. He received worship in a human way from His human friend, and He talked to His human friend in a very intimate and personal way. Abraham's worship of God in Genesis 18 was well-pleasing to God. Abraham and Jehovah's talking together like intimate friends is the best worship, the best prayer.

In one of the beginning meetings with the new ones, we need to let them know that the real worship to God is to talk to Him as our friend. We need to tell them that the very God has our human nature and that He is the same as we are. Furthermore, they need to realize that we are sons of God who have the divine life and the divine nature, so we are the same as He is. He is divine and human, and we are human and divine. Thus, we can have an intimate conversation, an intimate contact, with our Triune God. God does not like us to merely see Him as the Almighty God. God desires us to realize that He is like us and that we are like Him. From the very beginning of man's creation before his fall, man was made in the image of God.

We need to make God known to the new ones. Do not go to the new homes and tell them, "Now let us worship God. He is the holy, Almighty God. He is so high, and we are so low. He is so great, and we are so small. Let us all kneel down." If we instruct the new ones in this way, we are similar to the Muslims. We need to take some time to explain to the new ones and to teach them to know God by talking to Him in an intimate way. The desire of God's heart is for man to worship Him in an intimate, friendly way. God is not happy with our worshipping Him with the concept that we are small, fearing God to the uttermost and bowing down to the great God. God wants us to enjoy Him as our food and our drink. When we go to the home meetings, we need to forget about the natural, religious way to meet as in Christianity. That way to meet is not scriptural.

The Worship of the Lord Jesus in the House of Simon the Leper

The proper worship of the Lord Jesus can also be seen

in the house of Simon the leper in Bethany where Mary, Martha, and Lazarus were (John 12:1-3; cf. Mark 14:3; Matt. 26:6-7). These dear saints were rendering the Lord Jesus the highest standard of worship, and the Lord was happy. This meeting in this house was composed of the cleansed sinners typified by Simon the leper. Martha was serving, Lazarus was testifying, and Mary was loving. While the religious service was continuing to be practiced in the temple, the Lord Jesus was sitting in the house of Simon the leper, receiving His believers' intimate, personal worship.

While the Lord Jesus was walking on this earth, a formal, religious, Judaic worship was going on in the temple. At that time did God prefer the Judaic worship in the temple or the worship that can be seen in the house of Simon the leper? In Simon the leper's house, there was no sacrifice, no burning of incense, and no showbread. By that time God was disgusted with the Judaic, religious worship by the priests according to formalities. Eventually in A.D. 70 the Lord allowed the Roman army under Titus to destroy Jerusalem with the temple, fulfilling the Lord's prophecy in Matthew 24:2 concerning the temple that there would not be one stone left upon another stone. The worship in religion and the worship in reality are in two different realms. Christianity has brought the church into the religious world, but today in the Lord's recovery we are endeavoring to enjoy the Lord by being rescued from Christianity.

Worshipping God by Enjoying Him

We must be deeply impressed that we should not perform in a religious or pious way. We need to be men of God who are talking to the Lord all the time. We need to live a life of calling on His name and talking to Him and bring this life into the meetings. Eventually, our life becomes our worship. We should worship the Lord in the way that we live; there should be no difference. Our meeting is an exhibition of our daily life. If Christ is not the content of our daily life, what we do in the meetings is a performance in which we are the actors. To meet in this way is a falsehood to God. We must be genuine in our worship. God likes our human worship in our human spirit.

Many of us may hold on to the concept of religious worship. Many Christians today prefer to have big meetings according to schedules with a proper pastor and choir clothed in long gowns. To have a big meeting with a pastor and a choir is the proper worship to God according to their concept. The worship in many cathedrals and chapels is religious, formal, and quiet. This is in contrast with a meeting in a home where the saints are declaring, "O Lord, Amen, Hallelujah! O Lord Jesus, You are my food. You are my drink. You are my enjoyment!" The Lord Jesus prefers that we eat Him, drink Him, enjoy Him. All the religious people would highly appraise the formal and quiet service. They might say that it is not right to make noise in the presence of God. But the Psalms tell us that we need to make a joyful noise unto the Lord (66:1; 81:1; 95:1-2; 98:4, 6; 100:1).

We have to drop Christianity's way to meet, which is the religious way. The new ones whom we meet with may already have Christianity's way to worship God in their concept. We have to spend time to bring them into the realization that the real worship of God is in our spirit and is a matter of enjoying Christ as our life and life supply, our food, our drink, and our everything. We have to tell the new ones that the more we enjoy the Lord, the more He is worshipped. The more we enjoy Him, the more we talk to Him, contact Him, in a friendly and intimate way, the more He will be happy. We enjoy the Lord by conversing with Him and opening our heart to Him. Our enjoying Him in such a way is well-pleasing and pleasant to Him. We worship God in the spirit, in life, in enjoying Him.

When the Lord's death was imminent, He enacted the New Testament by establishing the Lord's table (Matt. 26:26-30). Concerning the bread of the Lord's table, the Lord said that this was His body and He told the disciples to take and eat in remembrance of Him. To eat Him is to remember Him, to worship Him. In like manner, the Lord charged us to drink the cup of the Lord's table in remembrance of Him. Thus, to drink Him is to worship Him. In John 4 the Lord Jesus indicated that drinking Him as the living water was the way to worship God. The Lord Jesus linked the drinking of Him and the worship of God together. These two items are one thing. The best way to worship God is to drink Him, to take Him as the living water. This real revelation of the true worship of God and the Lord Jesus must revolutionize our entire concept. As long as we have such a realization with a revolutionized concept concerning the worship of God and the Lord Jesus, we will know how to set up home meetings.

LEADING AND PROMOTING EACH ONE OF THE ATTENDANTS TO LEARN TO TAKE PART IN THE ACTIVITIES IN THE MEETINGS

We need to lead and promote each one of the attendants in the home meetings to learn to take part in the activities in the meetings. We need to take the lead, but we should not do everything for everybody. When the new ones in the home meetings follow our lead, we need to promote. We should not say to the new believers, "Let us sing Hymn #49." This is the wrong way. We should not call a hymn, but it is good to say, "May we sing a hymn?" When they say yes, we should ask, "Who will select the hymn?" or "What number would you like to sing?" Let them select and call the hymn.

If you do everything in the first few meetings with the new believers, they will consider you as a pastor who goes to their home to conduct a worship service to God. Do not say, "Please let us read John 3:16." If you feel that it is the right time to read some verses, propose this matter to them. You should say, "Would you like to read some verses?" When they respond that they would, you should not say, "Let us read John 3:16." Ask them what they would like to read. They may want to read the last verse of Revelation 22. Do not say to them, "Let's not read that verse because it does not suit today's meeting." Say "Amen" to what they want to do. Let them read the verse they choose. By doing this, you will be practicing to promote each one of them to learn to take part in the activities in the meetings. You may have a burden to read John 3:16, but it is better to drop the reading of this verse and let the new ones decide what to read. The environment may indicate that your burden for this verse was not of the Lord. If it was of the Lord, someone would surely say, "Let us read John 3:16." You have to believe in the Lord. You have to believe that the Lord is moving in the reading of the verses. Do not make up your mind to read certain verses in a definite and sure way. Leave the entire meeting in the hand of the Holy Spirit.

You may feel that to conduct the home meeting in this way is to make the meeting a mess. But it is not bad to have a mess. I am a person who likes to have everything in order, but when three of my grandchildren come to visit me, they make a mess of things. When they come to my house, they may get into mischief, but I am always pleased to see them. If they do not come back after a period of time, I miss them and expect them to come back again. I believe that my heart toward my grandchildren is somewhat like God's heart toward the new believers. If my little grandsons were trembling and fearful of offending me when they came to my house, that would not make me happy. When they are so energetic and full of life, my wife and I are happy and full of joy. Most grandparents like to have their grandchildren come to "bother" them. My grandchildren's "bothering" is quite pleasant to me. God also needs some enjoyment and happiness from His children.

Our God is not only divine but also very human. He partook of the human nature, and He likes to receive the human worship. We must worship God according to His economy. The religious way to meet of Christianity puts aside God's economy. It makes everything formal, scheduled, and dead. Christianity is full of formalities. The Lord Jesus did not meet with people in that way when He was on this earth.

We need to lead the attendants into the practice of

THE WAY TO BUILD UP HOME MEETINGS

selecting hymns, singing hymns, praying, reading and pray-reading the holy Word, giving testimonies, and fellowshipping one with another. By leading the attendants into such a practice, we will set a good example for them to follow and copy. We should not give orders but make suggestions to the attendants that they may learn to take the initiative in the activities in the meetings. Let the new ones do things and let them take the initiative in all the activities in the meetings.

FUNCTIONING AS ONE AMONG THE ATTENDANTS

We should also take the chance to give words of life supply occasionally, not as a pastor, a preacher, or a teacher, but as one of the attendants. We should not make ourselves another class of people in the home meetings. Finally, we need to take the chance to pray and to call a hymn at the right juncture as one among the attendants. We need to take the fellowship in this chapter and put it into practice. Then we will have good home meetings according to the heart's desire of our God and of our Lord Jesus.

Chapter Fourteen
THE STANDARD OF HOME MEETINGS

Scripture Reading: Matt. 24:14; Luke 17:20-21; John 3:3, 5; Eph. 3:8-11

In the Lord's recovery our preaching, teaching, and home meetings must come up to the high standard revealed in the New Testament. After visiting people by knocking on their doors, leading them to receive the Lord, and baptizing them, we should return to these new ones again and again to meet with them in their homes. These meetings will afford us the adequate time to bring them up to such a high standard.

THE HIGH STANDARD OF THE GOSPEL

We need to preach the high gospel revealed in the New Testament. In the New Testament, different terms are used for the gospel, such as the gospel of grace (Acts 20:24), the gospel of God (Rom. 1:1; 15:16), the gospel of Christ (Rom. 15:19), the gospel of Jesus Christ (Mark 1:1), **the gospel of the glory of Christ** (2 Cor. 4:4), **the gospel of peace** (Eph. 6:15), and the gospel of our salvation (Eph. 1:13). The gospel of the kingdom (Matt. 4:23) includes not only forgiveness of sins (cf. Luke 24:47) and the impartation of life (cf. John 20:31), but also the kingdom of the heavens (Matt. 24:14). In Ephesians 3:8 Paul said that he preached the unsearchable riches of Christ as the gospel. When I was young, I heard much concerning the gospel of grace and the forgiveness of sins, but I never heard of the gospel of the kingdom. Even for many years in the Lord's recovery, we did not see the gospel of the unsearchable riches of Christ.

The Gospel of the Kingdom

To enter into the kingdom of God, that is, to enter into the divine kingdom, we must be regenerated with the divine life. To enter into any kingdom, we must have the life of that kingdom. To enter into the animal kingdom, the animal life is needed. As human beings we have the human life, which ushers us into the human kingdom. Likewise, without the divine life, there is no way to enter into, to see, the divine kingdom (John 3:3, 5). We must preach the gospel of the kingdom of God that people may receive the divine life and be brought into the realm of the divine reign in the divine life. The gospel of the kingdom is to bring us into the realm, the sphere, of God's ruling.

The sphere of God's rule is in the divine life. Life rules, or controls. The life of a fruit-bearing tree controls the shape of its fruit. The fruit of an apple tree will be in the shape of an apple, and the fruit of a peach tree will be in the shape of a peach. As the different lives grow, they produce different fruits in different shapes. The fruit is shaped by the rule, or control, of the inner life and not by an outward mold. A tiger grows in the form of a tiger, while a man grows in the form of a man. The life of the tiger and the life of man control and determine their outward forms. As men who have been regenerated, we have received the life on the highest plane, the divine life. As this life grows within us we are being conformed to the image of God's Son (Rom. 8:29).

For us to be in the kingdom there is the need of a life on the highest plane (John 3:3, 5). In Genesis 1 and 2 there are different levels of life. God created the plant life, then the animal life, and finally, God created man. Man is the highest life created by God. In the second chapter of Genesis there is the divine life, the uncreated life, indicated by the tree of life (v. 9). The divine life is higher than the human life, the human life is higher than the animal life, and the animal life is higher than the plant life. The divine life, the life of lives, is the life on the highest plane. We are men possessing the human life, but God's intention is to transfer us into His divine life, making us divine. This divine life has brought us into the divine kingdom, and this divine life keeps us living in the divine realm.

This life reigns within us to shape us into the image of

God that we may express Him. The kingdom of God is the Lord Himself as the seed of life sown into His believers (Mark 4:3, 26) to develop into God's ruling realm. The divine reign in the divine life is revealed in Luke 17:20-21 where the Lord Jesus told us that this divine reign cannot be seen outwardly. Although this divine reign is not physically visible, we do have the reality of the divine reign within us, which is God's life reigning in our life. We must preach such a gospel of the kingdom to the whole inhabited earth (Matt. 24:14).

The Gospel of the Unsearchable Riches of Christ

All the riches of Christ's being and of Christ's doing compose the gospel of the unsearchable riches of Christ (Eph. 3:8). This gospel brings us into these riches that we may enjoy and participate in them. All these unsearchable riches of Christ become our constitution. As genuine Christians, we are wonderful constitutions of all the items of what Christ is. All the items of what Christ is and all that He has done, is doing, and will do for us are innumerable and are included in the unsearchable riches of Christ preached to us as the very gospel for our participation that we may daily enjoy Him. Whatever we enjoy of Christ is an item of this gospel. We need to preach this gospel in the new ones' homes. We should read Ephesians 3:8 to them, dwell on it, and spend some time to pray-read it with them until they become impressed and realize that as Christians they may daily enjoy the riches of Christ's being and doing.

Christ is God (Rom. 9:5), and Christ is man (Matt. 16:13). Christ is the Creator (Heb. 1:10), the Redeemer (Gal. 3:13), the Lord (Acts 2:36), the Master (Jude 4); Christ is life (John 14:6), Christ is light (John 8:12), and He is our righteousness, sanctification, and redemption (1 Cor. 1:30). Eventually, Christ is everything. Colossians 2:16-17 shows us that all positive things are a shadow of Christ. The air that we breathe, our drink, the food we eat, our clothing, house, and all our daily necessities are only shadows, but Christ is the body of these shadows. He is our real air

(John 20:22), our real food (6:35), our real drink (7:37-39; 4:14), our real clothing (Gal. 3:27), and our real lodging, our dwelling place (John 15:5). Christ is the tree (Gen. 2:9; John 15:1), the lion (Rev. 5:5), the ox, and the eagle (Ezek. 1:10). Christ is the Father (Isa. 9:6), the Son (Matt. 16:16), the Spirit (2 Cor. 3:17), and Jehovah (John 8:24; cf. Exo. 3:14-15). Christ is everything to us. Christ is all the members of the new man and in all the members (Col. 3:11). Paul said, "It is no longer I who live, but Christ lives in me" (Gal. 2:20), and "For to me to live is Christ" (Phil. 1:21). We must learn to know, to experience, and to enjoy these riches continually. O the depth of the riches of Christ! (Rom. 11:33).

The Gospel concerning the Economy of the Mystery Hidden in God

We must also have the high standard of the gospel concerning the economy of the mystery hidden in God (Eph. 3:9-11). The entire universe is a mystery, but within this mystery there is a deeper mystery which has been hidden in God. This deeper mystery is the purpose, the meaning, and the significance of this universe. This mystery was not known to man but was revealed to the apostles, especially to the Apostle Paul. Thus, Paul told us that he preached not only the unsearchable riches of Christ but also the economy of this mystery hidden in God from the ages. Economy is an anglicization of the Greek word *oikonomia,* denoting an arrangement, an administration, a plan, a purpose. God desired something, so He formed an arrangement, administration, plan, or purpose to gain it for Himself. What God desires is to gain a group of people to contain Him that they may become the members of the Body of Christ, that Christ may be their life, their Head, and their manifestation, and that they and He could be one universal new man to express Christ as the embodied God to fulfill His eternal purpose. The mystery of God is Christ, the mystery of Christ is the church, and Christ and the church are the great mystery (Eph. 5:32) hidden in God from the centuries and revealed to the Apostle Paul.

THE STANDARD OF HOME MEETINGS 127

Paul preached the divine economy as the very gospel. Ephesians 3:8 reveals the gospel of the unsearchable riches of Christ, while verse 9 reveals the gospel of the economy of the mystery hidden in God from the ages. We must realize, experience, and preach this economy to the new ones as the high standard of the gospel. Many Christians enjoy the gospel of grace, and some enjoy the gospel in the aspect of life, but few among today's Christians enjoy the gospel of the kingdom by being under the divine ruling in the divine life. Few enjoy the gospel of the unsearchable riches of Christ and the gospel of the economy of the mystery hidden in God from the ages.

To enjoy the gospel concerning the economy of the mystery hidden in God is to enjoy the church life, the life of the Body of Christ. I can testify that I am enjoying the universal church life. When I come to the United States, I enjoy the Body life, and when I go to Stuttgart or the Far East I enjoy this life. We must realize that we are in the enjoyment of the highest gospel, the gospel of the arrangement of the divine mystery—Christ and His Body. As I contact some dear saints, I realize that they do not have the real enjoyment of the universal church life of the Body of Christ. We need to enjoy the Body life, not only in knowledge but also in experience. I daily enjoy the support from the Body.

Praise the Lord that on this earth there is the Body, the universal grapevine (John 15:1, 4). This grapevine has spread all over the globe. In 1970 I was invited to New Zealand, and while passing through Australia, I stayed in Sydney and Melbourne. I felt lonely because at that time there was no church life there for me to enjoy. But today if I went to Sydney and Melbourne, I would enjoy the church life. I do not like to go anywhere where there is no church. I like to go to Taipei, Stuttgart, and Tokyo because of the lovable church life there. The enjoyment of the church life is the enjoyment of the highest gospel of the divine economy. The people in the world do not know the meaning of human existence, but we know because we enjoy the church life around the globe. While I was flying from Los Angeles to Tokyo, I was happy because I knew I would meet some dear brothers at the airport. I am happy to go to Brazil because so many there have all become my brothers. We may not know each other's language, but we are happy to be in the church. The church life around the globe is the gospel.

The highest enjoyment on this earth is the enjoyment of the church life. If there were no church on this earth, I would not care to be here. The corrupted earth is ugly and bothersome, but I like to be here because the church is here. The church life is our enjoyment, but it is only a foretaste. The New Jerusalem will be the full taste of the enjoyment of the glorious church life. The highest gospel is the gospel of Christ with the church. We must value, appreciate, and treasure the church. We enjoy the church life as the highest standard of the gospel. The highest preaching of the gospel is to bring to light God's economy hidden in Him from the ages.

The gospel concerning the economy of the mystery hidden in God is to produce the church for God's expression and glorification according to God's eternal plan, or purpose. The church is so lovable because it is the very expression and glorification of God. When God has the church, He is expressed and He is glorified. We need to enjoy God in His expression and in His glorification in such a high standard.

THE HIGH STANDARD OF THE MESSAGES

In the home meetings, we must have the high standard of the messages. When you go to the home meetings, do not teach low things; you must teach the higher truths. For this we should use the *Life Lessons*, the *Truth Lessons*, and the Life-study of the Scriptures. In these materials is the high standard of the truth, which is the processed Triune God for our enjoyment. The processed Triune God is not the "raw" God, but the "cooked" God for our enjoyment. To cook is to prepare food for eating by means of the process of heating. Through the Triune God's wonderful process, He has been "cooked" for us to eat and enjoy. We must learn to preach, to teach, and to fellowship the high standard of God's Word.

THE HIGH STANDARD OF HYMNS

For the home meetings we also need the high standard of hymns. The hymns must be high in significance and in expression. Hymn #501, "O glorious Christ, Savior mine," is a hymn of a high standard. When I was young, I was taught the song, "Jesus loves me this I know, for the Bible tells me so." Even the unbelievers were able to sing that hymn, and some young boys on the street would mockingly sing it to the Christians. This short hymn is good, but too low. Our hymnal, entitled *Hymns*, was compiled in 1964 with one thousand and eighty selected hymns; two hundred sixty-eight more have since been added. We have had these hymns for over twenty years, but we have mainly used those which were written by ourselves. Nevertheless, all those hymns were included, and a detailed table of contents was composed in a proper theological way. After reading the table of contents, one could realize that we do have a proper understanding of theology.

THE HIGH STANDARD OF PRAYER

In addition to the high standard of hymns for the home meetings, we must also have the high standard of prayer, both in word and in spirit.

THE HIGH STANDARD OF HEALING AND CASTING OUT OF DEMONS

We also need the high standard of healing and casting out of demons. Fifty years ago in north China we conducted healing and casting out of demons, but we did not do it in a low way. When we healed people, we healed them in the sense of the divine life. The healing was not simply to recover the sick ones' health, but to impart life into them according to 1 John 5:16. When you minister life to a sick one, he will not only be healed but also supplied with the divine life.

Furthermore, we must cast out the demons in the sense

of the divine authority. On one occasion in Chefoo, some brothers cast out seven demons from one person. On the commandment of the brothers, each demon spoke his name before leaving the person. The best way to know the authority of the Lord Jesus and the power of His name is to cast out demons. When you cast out demons, you can see how powerful the name of the Lord Jesus is, how much power the name of the Lord Jesus conveys, and you can see the Lord's authority. Do not do anything in a low way. Do everything in the highest standard, either in the sense of life or in the sense of authority. When you go out to knock on doors and you find sickness, pray for the healing of the sick ones at their request. When you see demon possession, do not hesitate, but immediately exercise your right to cast out the demons in the name of the Lord Jesus.

CHAPTER FIFTEEN

ABSOLUTE FOR GOD'S ORDAINED WAY

Scripture Reading: Acts 28:31; Luke 10:1-6; Acts 2:46; 5:42; Luke 9:59-60; Rom. 12:1; Eph. 6:18; Gal. 5:26; Heb. 12:1; 1 John 2:15-17; Acts 13:52; 2 Cor. 5:10; Matt. 25:19

LIVING TO GOD FOR THE SPREADING OF HIS KINGDOM

In the foregoing chapters, we have seen a clear vision of God's ordained way to practice the New Testament economy. Upon seeing such a vision, we should be absolute for this vision. We must be absolute for God's ordained way, living to God for the spreading of His kingdom. The four Gospels are a record of the completion of Christ, and the book of Acts records the propagation of Christ for the spread of the kingdom of God. At the end of Acts, Paul spoke to people in a desperate way concerning the kingdom of God (28:23, 31). The first five books of the New Testament conclude with Paul proclaiming the kingdom of God. If we have believed into God, our goal must be to live to God for the spreading of His kingdom.

First, we need to visit people at their homes for the seeking of God's chosen sons of peace (Luke 10:1-6). God in eternity chose many people to be sons of peace, yet God's selection needs our going out to visit people that these chosen ones can be found and brought to God. Then we must also go out to build up home meetings with the believers for the teaching of the truth, the edification of the believers, and the establishment of the local churches in view of the building up of the Body of Christ (Acts 2:46; 5:42).

Throughout the centuries, the Lord has recovered many items which were lost in His economy. In the past two and one half years the Lord has shown us that to visit people, to baptize them into the name of the Triune God, to set up home meetings, to build up these homes, and to establish local churches with a view to building up the Body of Christ is the Lord's present move. According to our own history and our investigation, there is no other way to practice the New Testament economy that is so high, so prevailing, and so effective.

Today the entire situation of Christianity is worsening and becoming more dead. This situation is not so prevailing, new, or living. But, we must realize that the Lord is coming and our time is very short. We should ask ourselves whether or not we should remain in the old way. If we do, we will surely delay the Lord's coming. If the Lord does not have His way with us, He may have to go to another people. But if He did go to another people, He would have to repeat what He has done with us over the past sixty years. This would surely hurt the Lord's heart. We must get into the Lord's heart and sympathize with Him, rising up to take His new way.

To oppose or criticize the new way of knocking on doors and setting up home meetings in the new believers' homes is foolish. What is wrong for believers to go out to visit people by knocking on their doors, baptizing them into the processed Triune God? Whether or not this way corresponds with your own idea concerning preaching the gospel, you cannot say that it is wrong. This way is not only right but also very much needed. There is the urgent need for all God's lovers to rise up to knock on people's doors to bring the processed Triune God into their homes, to minister and impart the processed Triune God into their being, and to bring them into an organic union with the processed Triune God by baptizing them. No church or leading one should prohibit others from taking this way or tell others to wait until the church is ready to practice this way. This is illogical and is like stopping a person from breathing until he is "ready" to do so. All the leaders of the churches around the globe should say "Amen" to this way, whether or not they agree with it. To stop or criticize this way is not wise. Let the saints have the freedom to go out on their own, team by team, to knock on doors. Even if the saints knock on doors every day, there is nothing wrong with this practice.

Several churches comprising about one thousand saints have been in Orange County, California for thirteen years, yet the total annual rate of increase has been only about two to three percent. There are many saints who love the Lord and His purpose, yet the increase has been pitifully low. However, in a little over a week's time in the 1987 summer training, more than three thousand seven hundred were baptized in Orange County through the saints going out to knock on doors primarily in the evenings. Even if only one fourth of these remain, there would be close to nine hundred believers who could form ten new churches in ten new localities.

We should be wise and not criticize, condemn, or oppose the new way. Rather, we should take the lead to rise up to go out to visit people in order to set up home meetings, and all the saints will follow. If we do well, the increase could be threefold each year, or at the very least, one hundred percent increase each year. Our practice in the past years was to have many big meetings each week in which message after message was given. We do not need to meet in that way any longer. We need to go out to others' homes, taking the dear name of Jesus into their homes. If the meetings are scattered, the saints will not die; rather, the saints will go to the homes with Jesus, the Bible, and salvation. There will be a great revival and a strong church life. We all must wake up and be revolutionized by going to the homes to preach and teach. Gradually, in city after city, churches will be raised up.

NO CONTROL BUT DEPENDENCE ON THE BODY

The elders must learn not to control; rather, they must learn to help the saints to grow, to promote their function, to develop their gift, and to cultivate their divine ability. Then all the saints will rise up to preach the gospel in a prevailing and effective way by knocking on people's doors, reading *The Mystery of Human Life,* helping people to believe, and baptizing them. At least once a week, or perhaps two or three times a week, the saints would build up the home meetings by teaching the new believers the truth, and by edifying them and helping them to grow in life, thus establishing the local church with a view to building up the Body of Christ.

The elders should not control, but encourage the saints to go to visit others. You may have had many experiences of the Lord, but those experiences may now be old. You should let the saints go out in a fresh way. Those who go out should learn to know the Body of Christ. On the one hand, the present leading ones should not control, giving the saints the full freedom. On the other hand, those who go out should learn never to be independent. You should always practice depending upon the Body. When you came into the church, you came in as a member of the Body, meeting in the church in your locality. You are not only a member of the Body of Christ universally, but you are also a member of the church in your locality. Therefore, you are subject not only to the Body, but also to the church in your locality. Do not do anything independently, but do everything in dependence on your local church with thorough fellowship. The church in a locality is a local expression of the Body of Christ. You must honor and respect the church in your locality. The leading ones should give you the full freedom, yet you must learn how to depend upon the church.

To go out without sufficient, adequate fellowship with the church is independent and divisive. There is only one Body on this earth. Regardless of how much we say that we are right, as long as we are independent of the church in our locality, we are divisive. We must not neglect the Body of Christ, the church with which we are meeting. As long as we have been meeting with the church for even a short time, we must realize that it is the local expression of the unique Body of Christ, and that we are members of this expression. On the one hand, all the leading ones should not control anybody, but on the other hand, everyone who really knows the Body of Christ should act, behave, and do things in a dependent way, realizing that we all are members of the same Body. Not only should the young ones depend on the older ones, but the older ones should also learn to depend upon the young ones because we are members of the same Body. If the hand in one's physical body said, "I trust in the head, but I have nothing to do with the arm," the arm said, "I have nothing to do with the neck," and the neck said, "I have nothing to do with the ear," all the members of this body would become detached. Every member in the body depends upon the circulation of the blood throughout the body. The circulation of the blood is not local or individualistic; it is universal and corporate. Independence from the Body is like cancer, a disease not of germs, but of cells which grow for their own purpose. Cancer cells can kill the whole body.

We are practicing the new way, and the new way is a way without control. Some of the more experienced ones may hesitate to say "Amen" to this way. They may consider that this way is risky and could result in division and confusion. They may desire to wait and see what will happen with the other churches who take this way. On the other hand, others, especially the young ones, may want to act independently of the church. If we go out independently from the church, after a short time we will be in division. With such an attitude, it will be dangerous for us to take the new way, risking a division that could seriously damage the Body. We all have to learn, on the one hand, not to control others, and on the other hand, to depend upon our brothers. We are not individualistic or detached members; we are attached members. We are a corporate Body, depending upon one another.

For one to consider that, since he brought the Lord's recovery to a certain place, he has the right to control the church there, is foolish. The elders of the churches must learn not to control. In the past twenty-five years the Lord through this ministry has raised up over six hundred churches in Central America, South America, North America, Africa, Europe, and Australasia. If I would have controlled the churches, this never could have happened. Today there are so many churches to testify that the way of no control is effective.

On the other hand, everyone must learn to be dependent, trusting the elders and the church where we meet. We should ask the elders to help us and go to them to thoroughly fellowship everything regardless of what attitude they would have and regardless of what they would say. As members of the Body, we should depend on the Body. Then we will have peace, we will have the enjoyment, and the Lord's blessing will be with us. Division and confusion exhaust the members of the Body, but if we practice fellowship and dependence on the Body, we will have a unanimous oneness in a condition of peace. May the Lord keep us in the genuine oneness and teach us to live such a oneness in His recovery.

BEING ABSOLUTE FOR SUCH A LIVING FOR OUR WHOLE LIFE

We must live to God for the spreading of His kingdom by visiting people and setting up home meetings, and we must be absolute for such a living for our whole life. We should take such a living as the purpose of life, whether we are job-dropping full-timers or money-making full-timers (Luke 9:59-60). We simply should have a job which can sustain us, provide a proper living for our family, and provide for a good upbringing and education for our children. Then we must use the rest of our ability, time, and resources for going out to knock on people's doors to baptize them into the Triune God and to set up home meetings to build up the churches. Every day, every week, every month, and every year throughout our whole life, we must go out to baptize people and set up home meetings. This should become our favorite pastime and even our "addiction." To be able to say at the Lord's return that thousands of people have been baptized into the Triune God through us and that many churches have been raised up through our home meetings will be a glory to us at the Lord's coming back. But if the Lord comes back and we are empty-handed, we will be troubled at His coming back.

Some may say that to do well at their job or to do well in school requires them to compete and that this competition can fully occupy their time. However, no occupation, regardless of the competition, is to such a high standard that it does not leave us any leisure time. If we have a proper heart, there is still enough time for us to live a life for the spreading of the kingdom. If in one week we do not baptize one person, at least after two weeks we can get one baptized. To go out once or twice a week for two hours is adequate to baptize one person and take care of the baptized ones by setting up meetings in their homes. These new ones will grow, and they will learn from us and repeat what we do. To go out in this way is for the spreading of the kingdom of God. The way of Christianity is to send their young people to the seminary to become professional pastors, the clergy, while all the others sit in their congregations doing nothing. This way will delay the Lord, but the new way will speed up the Lord's return. There is no excuse for our not taking the spreading of the kingdom of God as the purpose of our life.

We must be vigilant every day without wasting our time, energy, and money. All of our time, our money, and our energy must be spent for the unique purpose of knocking on people's doors and setting up home meetings. We must also be vigilant in consecration (Rom. 12:1). Many years ago we may have consecrated ourselves to the Lord, but we must remain in that consecration today. We need to be vigilant in prayer (Eph. 6:18) and in dealing with self-seeking, sins, and worldliness (Gal. 5:26a; Heb. 12:1; 1 John 2:15-17). Also, we must be vigilant in being filled, saturated, and empowered by the Spirit (Acts 13:52) every day and every moment. We must be vigilant in bringing people to Christ and building up home meetings. If we have not baptized one person in two weeks, we need to consider why and not let our time pass away. Then if we go out in full desperation, we will see at least one baptized. We must take the spreading of the kingdom of God as our real and unique career.

If we are vigilant in consecration, in prayer, in dealing with self-seeking, sins, and worldliness, in being filled, saturated, and empowered by the Spirit, in bringing people to Christ and building up home meetings, and in taking the spreading of the kingdom of God as our real career, we will be ready to meet the Lord at His judgment seat (2 Cor. 5:10; Matt. 25:19). Every day we should live before the judgment seat of Christ, being fearful that if the Lord comes, we may not be ready to meet Him. It is more than worthwhile for us to rise up and go out to knock on people's doors to get them baptized. Then we need to set up home meetings and build them up by teaching the new ones the truth and edifying them with a view to building up the Body of Christ. May the Lord bless us in our divine appointment to bear fruit for the producing of His Body (John 15:16).

CHAPTER SIXTEEN

ONE WAY FOR ONE GOAL

Scripture Reading: Mark 16:15; Matt. 28:19; Acts 5:42; Eph. 4:11-12; Rev. 21:2; 1 Tim. 1:3-4; Acts 2:42; 1 Tim. 6:3; Eph. 3:9

ONE WAY FOR ONE GOAL IN THE GOSPELS AND ACTS

Every point of the final four chapters of this book is crucial and vital to our present situation in the Lord's recovery. In this chapter we want to see the matter of having one way for one goal. We must be deeply impressed that what is revealed in the four Gospels plus Acts is the one way to carry out God's one goal. In the four Gospels, God's Christ was completed. Then in the Acts this completed Christ of God was propagated. The spread of God's kingdom was taking place according to God's economy, and this spreading is by one way. There are not two ways to practice the New Testament economy revealed in the first five books of the New Testament. The one completed Christ was preached and propagated for the spreading of the kingdom of God by one way according to God's eternal economy.

There is one way to carry out God's unique goal. The saints in the early church life in the book of Acts were endeavoring to reach the one unique goal to complete God's eternal economy. This one unique goal is the building up of the Body of Christ that God may have a corporate expression on the earth with a view to the coming New Jerusalem as God's eternal corporate expression (Rev. 21:2). The New Jerusalem is the total conclusion of the sixty-six books of the divine revelation and is the eternal goal in God's eternal economy. There is only one way to reach this goal. Peter was in this way with all his co-workers, and many of the saints at his time were in this way. Then Paul continued in this way with all his co-workers and with many Gentile believers. Paul's co-worker, Barnabas, was in this one way for a while, and he was the one who brought Paul into this one way (Acts 9:26-27; 11:22-26). He and Paul were laboring in this one way until he dissented from Paul (Acts 15:35-39). After this incident Barnabas no longer appears in the divine record in Acts of the Lord's move in God's New Testament economy. After the record of Barnabas's contention with Paul in Acts 15, we read the names only of Paul and his co-workers. Barnabas's name is not mentioned again in the Acts. To be mentioned in the divine record positively, one had to take the one way for God's one, unique goal.

PREFERENCES, OPINIONS, AND DIFFERENT TEACHINGS CAUSING DIVISIONS

The Epistles show us that different ways crept in among the saints and the churches. The first Epistle in the New Testament is the book of Romans, which is concerning the Christian life for the church life. At the end of this Epistle, Paul warned the believers to "keep a watchful eye on those who make divisions and causes of falling contrary to the teaching which you have learned" (16:17). The first chapter after Romans 16 in the New Testament is 1 Corinthians 1. This chapter of the New Testament shows us that divisions came into the church through different preferences (vv. 10, 12). Some of the saints preferred Paul's ministry, others preferred Apollos's ministry, and still others preferred Cephas's ministry. These different, personal preferences brought in different ways. The different ways produced by man's preferences and opinions always cause divisions.

Not only did different opinions and preferences come into the church life but also different teachings. In 1 Timothy 1:3-4 Paul charged Timothy to remain in Ephesus with the one purpose of charging certain ones not to teach differently. According to these verses to teach differently is to teach things that are not according to God's economy. Verse 3 speaks of different teachings, and verse 4 speaks of God's economy. God's economy is the unique thing in the

ONE WAY FOR ONE GOAL   141

Lord's recovery. What we preach and teach should be God's economy. We should not stress anything other than God's economy. To stress anything other than God's economy is to teach differently. The truth of baptism is a part of God's economy, but if this truth is stressed apart from God's economy, it will cause division. The matter of baptism has caused divisions in today's Christendom. The Presbyterians practice baptism by sprinkling while the Baptists practice baptism by immersion. Even among those who believe in baptism by immersion there are different concepts concerning the method of baptism. Divisions have been produced by the different ways, opinions, and arguments concerning baptism. All the different ways for Christians to serve and to do work for God have caused divisions. Whatever is recorded in the holy revelation of the divine Word is something concerning God's economy. But many of these items have been stressed apart from God's economy, and many of the Lord's children have stressed different items according to their personal preference or taste. The result has been division after division.

In the early 1800s under the leadership of John Nelson Darby, the Brethren in England were raised up. Through the Brethren, the Lord was able to unlock many of the truths in His holy Word, and what the Lord accomplished through them was marvelous. Within a short period of time, however, the Brethren were divided again and again. Even while Darby was still alive, there was a division between him and Benjamin Newton. There was also a division between Darby and George Müller, who became famous for his work with orphans and his living by faith. Today there are many divisions among the Brethren. One sister who grew up in a Brethren family told me that the assembly she met with was divided into two assemblies over whether to use certain musical instruments in their worship service.

I came to the United States near the end of 1962 to begin the ministry, and the Lord began to move and spread. In the church in Los Angeles, there was a substantial increase. Among the believers whom the Lord was gathering in Los Angeles were four different groups: the brothers who had been in the recovery for years from China, the saints who followed the famous writers of the inner life line, the saints who came out of the Brethren, and the saints who were Pentecostal. One evening in Glendale, California, in the home of a Pentecostal brother, we were all meeting together, and the saints were happy. They were shouting and singing. Suddenly one of the brothers from the Pentecostal group proposed that all of the four different groups come together. All the saints happily said "Amen" to this proposal. They all turned to me for a response, but I was very sober.

I told them that it was very good for Christians to come together and that every Christian who loves the Lord wants to practice the Body life revealed in Romans 12. At that time the Body ministry was a popular term among many believers. I admonished them that anyone who wanted to practice the Body life according to Romans 12 needed to go on to Romans 14. Romans 14 tells us how we need to receive the believers according to God's receiving and not according to doctrinal concepts. In verses 2 and 3 of this chapter Paul says, "One believes that he may eat all things, but he who is weak eats vegetables. Let not him who eats despise him who does not eat, and let not him who does not eat judge him who eats, for God has received him." Verses 5 and 6 say, "One judges one day above another, another judges every day alike. Let each be fully persuaded in his own mind. He who observes the day, observes it to the Lord; and he who eats, eats to the Lord, for he gives thanks to God; and he who does not eat, to the Lord he does not eat, and gives thanks to God." Paul wrote this to the saints in Rome so that they would not be divided over doctrinal concepts and preferences. They had preferences in diet and preferences in keeping days. I pointed this out to the saints who wanted to come together, and I questioned them about the matter of speaking in tongues. I asked them if those who spoke in tongues would be willing to receive those who did not speak in tongues, and if those who did not speak in tongues would be willing to receive those who did. They responded that they were willing to do this. Everyone was happy, and they declared that they were all one in Christ. They agreed to come together, but I admonished them not to forget my word concerning Romans 12 and 14.

I was able to be with the saints on the first Lord's Day that they met together, and this meeting was very good. In a sense, that meeting was like a wedding day in which everyone was happy. The following Lord's Day, I was away and could not meet with the saints. That Monday, I received a phone call from one of the brothers from the Brethren group. He said that he was unhappy about the Pentecostal activities in the meeting. The Pentecostal saints brought in their tambourines, and this offended the orthodox Brethren. When I came back to Los Angeles, this brother from the Brethren group told me that I had to do something about the tambourines in the meeting. This brother had no problem with having a piano in the meetings so I asked him, "In the eyes of God, what is the difference between a tambourine and a piano?" He responded that there was no difference in the eyes of God, but he still insisted that he did not like tambourines in the meeting. Eventually, these groups disbanded. Many of the saints could not stay in oneness because they could not give up their preference, their choice, their taste. This story illustrates the real situation of today's Christianity. If each one of us practices according to his choice and his taste, how can we go on together? We must take one way for one goal.

From the very beginning of the recovery in 1922, we never changed the one way or the one goal. We have only had one way for one goal. The Lord's recovery has suffered from different people's opinions. Some brothers tried to take the way of the Lord's recovery, but they eventually began to express their opinions. They came to the Lord's recovery, and then they left because they wanted to take their own way. In order for us to be preserved in the Lord, we need to see the one way for the one goal.

THE CONTROLLING FACTOR OF THE ONE WAY

We need to see that the Lord's new way is the one way, the God-ordained way, and this way is to visit people for the preaching of the gospel and to establish home meetings for the building up of the church (Mark 16:15; Matt. 28:19; Acts 5:42). From the beginning of the Lord's recovery in mainland China, we studied the Bible and the history of the church thoroughly so that we could see the proper practice of the church life. Brother Nee set forth the proper practice of the church life in his book *The Normal Christian Church Life*. We have said that we are taking the Lord's new way, but actually this new way is an ancient way. Peter and Paul both took this way, and we are following them to take the same way.

The way of Christianity is the way of confusion. Confusion prevails in Christianity. We are living in the midst of this confusion, but we have been brought into the Lord's recovery through His mercy to practice the one way to carry out His New Testament economy. In this new way, there should be no control. No one needs to get someone's permission or approval to visit others by knocking on their doors. Because of the new way, however, there is an open door for us to think that we are free to do whatever we desire. We need to be impressed that we have only one way, and that this one way is the controlling factor among us.

THE GOD-ORDAINED WAY BEING THE MOST EFFECTIVE WAY

Some saints have been in the Lord's recovery for many years. They love the recovery and the church to the uttermost. When I began to share about visiting people for the preaching of the gospel and establishing home meetings, however, they were concerned about dropping our old way of meeting. Our old way of meeting was a production of the traditional practice of Christianity. We practiced to have big meetings all the time with big speakers delivering good messages. I pointed out to the saints who have been with us for many years that there is nothing wrong with having big meetings on the Lord's Day with a good message given by a good speaker. Many of them had been listening to good messages for over thirty years, but I asked them how much fruit they had born in the years that they had been listening to those good messages. Some told me that they had brought ten to the Lord within the many years they had been in the church life. Then I told them to look at the actual situation today. When I left Taipei in 1961, the number of saints there was over twenty thousand. When I came back twenty-three years later, there were less than eleven thousand saints. I asked the saints who said that they had brought some to the Lord during the years they had been in the church life, where these ones were today.

Our old way to practice the church life may be good, but it is deadening. We must not take that way. When we are driving a car down the street and realize that it is a dead end, we will turn back. None of us would be foolish enough to keep driving through a dead end. When we see a dead end sign, we need to make a u-turn. Our old way to practice the church life is a dead end. We must take the new way, the God-ordained way, to practice the New Testament economy.

In the last two terms of the full-time training in Taipei, twenty-four thousand people have been baptized. Those who meet in the halls in Taipei are less than four thousand, but outside the halls there are over eight thousand meeting in homes. The number of saints meeting in the homes in Taipei is increasing. There are thousands of homes with small groups of saints worshipping God, preaching the gospel, teaching the truth, breaking bread, and fellowshipping one with another. All these home meetings make the Lord happy. These facts along with our history are convincing and subduing. Within ten years, I expect that there will be ten thousand homes meeting in Taipei.

Recently one young sister among us went out to visit people for close to a week without getting anyone baptized. She fasted, repented, and cried out to the Lord for a breakthrough. When she went out the next evening, she baptized six people. Her fasting prayer was heard by the

Lord, and she gained six new ones. The God-ordained way to practice the New Testament economy is the unique way, the biblical way, and the most effective way. If we love the Lord and do not want to take the Lord's new way, we are foolish. The Lord Jesus did tell us, however, that no one who has drunk the old wine desires the new, for he says that the old is better (Luke 5:39). Actually, the new wine is better. When we get into the taste of knocking on doors to turn people to believe and be baptized, we will become addicted to this gospel service. When we establish home meetings and see the new ones growing in the divine life, we will be happy. These new ones whom we have baptized will be like our children whom we love and care for. We will be like nursing mothers (1 Thes. 2:7) who enjoy seeing their children grow. One leading one in the United States who was a trainee in the full-time training in Taipei told me he became addicted to knocking on people's doors to get them baptized and to setting up and having home meetings.

PRESENTING THE TRUTH
TO THE NEW ONES IN LARGE GATHERINGS

All the new ones who have come into the Lord's recovery through door knocking and through home meetings occasionally need to hear a proper message of truth related to the vision of the Lord's recovery. The whole church needs to come together to give the Lord an opportunity to solidly root the new ones through their hearing of a proper message of God's revelation. Providing the new ones with a vision cannot be done properly or adequately in small homes. We need the big meetings to perform this task. The new ones can meet in the homes during the week, and once a month they can come together to hear a proper message on God's economy and on God's divine revelation. In this way all the new ones will be solidly rooted and founded in truth. Some brothers need to give messages on the Lord's recovery, on God's economy, and on the divine revelation. They have to learn the truth and learn how to present the truth in a proper way in the

Lord's unique New Testament ministry. In the Old Testament there was only one ministry, the ministry of the law, and in the New Testament there is only one ministry, the ministry of the Spirit, the ministry of life, the ministry of righteousness (2 Cor. 3:6-9). We all are working for God's purpose in this one ministry, so we have one way for one goal by one ministry.

ONE WAY FOR ONE GOAL WITHOUT OPINION AND WITHOUT DIFFERENT TEACHINGS

The one goal in the Lord's recovery is not merely for the spreading of the gospel, not merely for the release of the biblical truths, not merely for saving sinners, and not merely for edifying the believers, but mainly for the building up of the Body of Christ that God may have a corporate expression on the earth, even in this age, for the building up of the coming New Jerusalem as God's eternal, corporate expression (Eph. 4:11-12; Rev. 21:2). We need to take this one way for one goal without opinion both in theory and in practice.

Furthermore, we take this one way for one goal without different teachings (1 Tim. 1:3-4). We take only the apostles' teaching (Acts 2:42) as the healthy words of the Lord Jesus (1 Tim. 6:3). First Timothy 1 speaks of the teaching concerning God's economy and chapter six speaks of the healthy words of the Lord Jesus. All the teachings of the apostles are for God's economy, and these teachings are the healthy words of the Lord Jesus. The apostles learned these words from the Lord and followed the Lord to teach the same thing that He did. The apostles' teaching is the teaching concerning God's economy. We must preach and teach concerning Christ's unsearchable riches and God's New Testament economy. In Ephesians 3:8 Paul speaks of the unsearchable riches of Christ as the gospel and in verse 9 he speaks of God's eternal economy. We must preach and teach these two items. May the Lord preserve us in the one way for one goal without opinion and without different teachings.

CHAPTER SEVENTEEN

THE APOSTLES' TEACHING AND FELLOWSHIP

Scripture Reading: Acts 2:42; 1 John 1:2-3; 2 Cor. 13:14; Phil. 2:1; Eph. 4:3-6; 2 John 9-11; 1 Tim. 1:3-4; Jude 3; Eph. 4:13; 1 Cor. 1:10

In this chapter we want to see the apostles' teaching and fellowship. Acts 2:42 says, "And they were continuing steadfastly in the teaching and the fellowship of the apostles, in the breaking of bread and the prayers." In this verse Luke uses the preposition "in" twice. The new ones who were saved on the day of Pentecost continued in two groups of things: in the teaching and fellowship of the apostles and in the breaking of bread and the prayers. Four items are divided into two groups. The teaching and the fellowship are related to the apostles, while the breaking of bread and the prayers are not related to the apostles. This means that a person who prays does not need to pray in something related to the apostles. If saints break bread, they do not need to break bread in something related to the apostles. But no one has the freedom in the divine economy to teach whatever he likes to teach. Our teaching must be restricted by the limit and by the sphere of the apostles' teaching. Furthermore, a fellowship outside the fellowship of the apostles is divisive. Our fellowship must be inside the fellowship of the apostles. The apostles' teaching is unique, and the apostles' fellowship is also unique. But the breaking of bread and prayer are not limited in the sphere of the apostles.

THE APOSTLES' TEACHING

In the previous chapter we saw that we should have one way for one goal. The one way for the one goal is altogether in the limit, in the sphere, of the apostles' teaching. All the problems, divisions, and confusion among the Christians today are due to one thing—not caring for the apostles' teaching. Many Christians teach something different from the apostles' teaching. They have not been limited, restricted, and kept strictly in the sphere of the apostles' teaching. The deciding factor of the one way for one goal is the apostles' teaching.

Many things are taught in Christendom that do not belong to or are not in the sphere of the apostles' teaching. Baptism by immersion is taught by some as the unique term and condition for receiving the saints. Although baptism by immersion is scripturally correct, to make it a term by which one receives the believers is altogether sectarian. Denominations are the result of different teachings other than the apostles' teaching. A denomination is a denominated sect, a sect with a name. When the Lord showed us the truth of the one Body of Christ and of divisions being of the flesh, we began to condemn the word denomination. A denomination is a sect that takes a name other than the name of the Lord Jesus Christ. Lutheran, Wesleyan, Anglican, Presbyterian, Baptist, and Episcopalian are names adopted by groups of Christians other than the unique name of the Lord Jesus Christ.

Baptism by immersion, which shows the real significance of being buried together with Christ (Rom. 6:4), is altogether scriptural, but to make this practice the unique condition for receiving the believers is absolutely sectarian. The presbytery, which is an anglicized Greek word referring to the body of elders or the eldership in a local church (1 Tim. 4:14), is a biblical truth. A local church is under the management and oversight of the elders. But to use the truth concerning the presbytery to denominate a group of believers, thus separating them from other believers, is a different and wrong teaching which causes division.

The Episcopal denomination gets its name from the Greek word *episkopos*, which means overseer, or bishop. An overseer in a local church is an elder (Acts 20:17, 28). But it was Ignatius in the second century who taught that an overseer, a bishop, is higher than an elder. From this erroneous teaching came the hierarchy of bishops, archbishops, cardinals, and the pope. This teaching is also the source of the episcopal system of ecclesiastical government. This episcopal system of government and the hierarchy of the Roman Catholic Church are unscriptural and abominable in the eyes of God. But even to use a certain practice which is scriptural to denominate a certain group is to make a division, to form a named, official sect. Denominations are absolutely wrong.

Christianity has many ways because of the many teachings outside the limit of the apostles' teaching. Anything other than the apostles' teaching should not be taught among Christians. What we should teach is only the teachings within the limit of the apostles' teaching. I once met a dear saint who asked me whether we in the churches practiced footwashing every time we had the Lord's table. I told this brother that we know footwashing is in the Bible and that we have practiced it, but not in a formal or legal way. He then said that our Lord's table was wrong because we did not practice footwashing when we had it. This brother's group taught footwashing as a term or a condition for taking the Lord's table. A teaching outside of the limit of the apostles' teaching always creates division. Even if today's tongue-speaking were proper, it still should not be a term or condition for us to fellowship with one another and to receive the saints. We should not make anything, even if that thing is scriptural, a term or a condition of fellowship with other saints. To practice in this way is to be sectarian. We can take one way only by keeping the apostles' teaching. Otherwise, we cannot have the one way.

When Paul told Timothy to charge certain ones not to teach differently he was referring to the teaching of myths, unending genealogies (1 Tim. 1:4), and the law (vv. 7-8). At Paul's time some Judaistic believers still taught others the genealogies and the law in the Old Testament. The law was the teaching of Moses, not the teaching of the Lord Jesus or the teaching of the apostles. If we teach anything which has never been taught by the Lord Jesus or the apostles, we are teaching something other than God's economy, something outside the apostles' teaching. A teaching other than the apostles' teaching will issue in division. We can have one way only by restricting our teaching to be within the limit of the apostles' teaching.

The apostles' teaching is the teaching concerning Christ's person and redemptive work (2 John 9-11). It is also the teaching concerning God's economy in faith (1 Tim. 1:3-4). God's economy is not to have a mission field for preaching the gospel or to have a Bible school to teach the truths. God's economy is to dispense or impart the Triune God into His chosen and redeemed people to be their life and everything that they might be regenerated and transformed into the proper material for the building up of the Body of Christ that God may have a corporate expression on the earth in many localities in this age with a view to the building up of the coming New Jerusalem for His eternal expression. If we limit ourselves to the apostles' teaching, the teaching concerning God's economy, we will be kept in oneness and will have one way for one goal. We must have a clear vision concerning God's economy; then we will never be misled. We will keep ourselves going toward the unique goal in the unique way.

The apostles' teaching is the believers' faith, belief, that is, what the believers believe in (Jude 3; Eph. 4:13). We believe in Jesus Christ, the Son of God, becoming the Son of Man. We believe in such a God-man as our life and Savior. We believe in His death for our sins and in His resurrection for us to have His divine life. We believe in His ascension, and we believe that today He is the life-giving Spirit, indwelling us to live in us that we may live Him. These items are the believers' faith, which is the teaching of the apostles. All doctrines other than this teaching of the apostles cause divisions among the believers (1 Cor. 1:10).

THE APOSTLES' FELLOWSHIP

Teaching creates fellowship. If I were to teach footwashing as a condition for receiving the saints, this

THE APOSTLES' TEACHING AND FELLOWSHIP   153

teaching would immediately produce a particular fellowship. Fellowship comes from the teaching. There should be only one unique teaching—the teaching of the apostles. Furthermore, there should be one unique fellowship which is produced by the apostles' teaching. What we teach will produce a kind of fellowship. If we teach wrongly and differently from the apostles' teaching, our teaching will produce a sectarian, divisive fellowship. If I teach baptism by immersion as a condition or a term for receiving the saints, this teaching will produce a Baptist fellowship. Many Baptist denominations will fellowship only with ones who have been baptized by a Baptist preacher in "Baptist water." If one has been baptized by someone else, that baptism is not official or does not count. Thus, we can see that wrong teaching produces wrong, divisive fellowship. We can have one way for one goal by keeping ourselves strictly in the limit of the apostles' teaching and the apostles' fellowship. There should not be another fellowship besides the apostles' fellowship.

In our work for the Lord, we must keep ourselves in the apostles' fellowship. If you have the burden to go to another locality to have the church life, you should do it with adequate fellowship from the church where you are. If you feel that you can raise up the church life in another city without fellowship with the brothers in the church in your locality, you will be raising up something outside the apostles' fellowship. The apostles' fellowship is universal in time and space. This fellowship includes all parts of the globe and includes all the centuries. Peter, Paul, and all the saints practicing the proper church life were in this fellowship. Anyone who would go out to another place to raise up the church life must have adequate fellowship with the church he has been meeting with. Otherwise, what he raises up will be something outside the apostles' fellowship and will cause division.

The principle of fellowship in the New Testament keeps us living the Body life. My hand cannot function in a detached way from the other members of my body. If my hand becomes detached, it is separated from the body.

Likewise, as members of the Body of Christ, we should not do things in a detached way. We have to learn to listen to one another. The proper fellowship is that we listen to one another. The hand listens to the arm, and the arm listens to the hand. The church in a locality should not be raised up by us independently without any fellowship with the source we came from. By keeping the principle of fellowship, we listen to one another. To listen to one another is to respect the Body. When the hand listens to the arm, the hand respects the body. To reject a member of the Body with whom you are connected, is to reject the Body itself. To disregard the Body and not listen to the Body is wrong.

Matthew 18 shows us that to refuse to hear the church is a very serious matter (v. 17). We must keep ourselves in the one way for the one goal by keeping ourselves in the proper fellowship of the Body of Christ, which is the unique oneness. The church in New York should not say, "We have nothing to do with the church in Los Angeles because all the churches are independent from one another." The churches are only independent from one another in the area of administration or management. Besides the matter of management, all the churches should depend upon one another. No church should be independent from the other churches. Once a local church becomes independent, it loses its identity and becomes a local sect. Whether or not a church is a local sect or a local church, depends upon what kind of fellowship it keeps.

All of us have the freedom to knock on people's doors and set up home meetings. Out of the home meetings we can raise up a local church. But if we do this independently without any relationship to any church, what we raise up will be an independent sect. A proper local church is related to other churches. We must remember that there are churches on this earth which are already in existence. The existence of a new church must be related to the churches that are preexisting. To have fellowship with the churches keeps us in the proper fellowship of the apostles, which means that we will be kept in the genuine oneness of the

Body of Christ. To preach the gospel, to baptize people, and to set up home meetings is not related to the apostles' fellowship. But to turn those home meetings into a local church in a certain locality is related to the apostles' fellowship. To have an independent fellowship in a locality is divisive. On the other hand, the leading brothers in the church should not control the saints. They should not have the attitude that the saints need to get their permission to raise up the church life in a certain place. For the leading brothers to ask the saints to get their permission is to exercise control over the saints. To practice this is not to keep the oneness of the fellowship of the apostles.

With the leading ones there should be no control, and with all the believers there should be no independence. We need the balance of no control and no independence. If the saints have the burden to go to raise up the church life, the leading ones should encourage them to do this and help them by giving them warning, advice, and instruction. The believers, on the other hand, should behave and have their entire being kept in fellowship with the existing church to keep them in the unique fellowship of the apostles. As we go out to knock on people's doors, baptize people, and set up home meetings, we must practice this fellowship. Otherwise, divisions will result. We must learn not to exercise control over anyone and not to practice being independent. In our physical body, there is no independence among the members. Likewise, in the Body of Christ independence cannot be practiced. Once we practice independence, we get ourselves into the dangerous state of being detached or separated from the Body.

The apostles' fellowship is with the Father and the Son (1 John 1:3) and is also the fellowship of the Spirit (2 Cor. 13:14), which the apostles participated in and ministered to the believers through the preaching of the divine life (1 John 1:2-3). Preaching produces fellowship, and fellowship must be of the divine life. The blood circulation in our physical body is crucial to our staying alive. This blood circulation is the fellowship of our physical life. If this fellowship is stopped, disease or death can result. Cancer cells are cells that are outside the "fellowship of the physical body." Today in the church, we must realize that if we are going to keep the proper fellowship, we must learn to live by the divine life. When we live by the divine life, we are in the circulation of the divine life, the fellowship.

Perhaps a certain brother has the burden to raise up the church life in another locality. The leading brothers may come to this brother to tell him that they need more fellowship. This brother then may respond, "What is wrong with my going to another city? Why do you have to come to check on me?" If this brother responds to the leading ones in this way, he is speaking by his natural life and not by the divine life. He needs a change of attitude. He should respond to the leading brothers from his spirit by the divine life by saying, "Brothers, I am happy that you want to have more fellowship with me. I also want to have more fellowship with you to receive your help." When this brother responds in such a way, he is speaking in the spirit by the divine life and conversing with the leading ones in the fellowship of the apostles. To say things and behave by our own life is to get out of the fellowship of the apostles. As long as we do things apart from the spirit and not with the divine life but with our natural life, we are outside of the fellowship of the apostles.

We need a vision of the apostles' teaching and fellowship to guide us, control us, and restrict us. "Where there is no vision, the people cast off restraint" (Pro. 29:18—ASV). Without such a vision, our work could issue in division. We should be in the teaching of the apostles and in the fellowship of the apostles. To keep ourselves in the fellowship of the apostles, we must live and behave in the divine life. All that we say and do must be the right thing in the right spirit with the right life, which is the divine life not our human life. Our human life may be ethical, moral, and proper, but it is still our natural life. If we walk in our natural life, we are outside the fellowship of the apostles. Then we may set up another fellowship that will create a division. To keep the one way for the one goal and to stay in the fellowship of the apostles, we must live and behave in the divine life. When we live and behave in the divine life, we keep ourselves in the teaching and fellowship of the apostles, and in this fellowship we will have one way for one goal. Then we will keep the oneness in the Lord's Body.

The apostles' fellowship is the fellowship in which the believers enjoy the divine life and through which they fellowship with one another in the spirit (Phil. 2:1; Acts 2:42). In the fellowship of the apostles, there is the enjoyment of the divine life. This fellowship is altogether a matter of the divine life in the mingled spirit. We need to do everything in our spirit with the divine life. This unique fellowship is the genuine oneness of the Body of Christ as the unique ground for the believers to be kept one in Christ (Eph. 4:3-6). You may go to another locality and say, "We are going to take the standing of the church." You may want to take the ground of the church, but by what life do you take the church ground? If you take the church ground by your natural life for your own standing, the ground on which you stand is the ground of division. The ground of the church must be the ground of oneness, and this oneness can only be kept by our being in the spirit with the divine life.

CHAPTER EIGHTEEN

THE NEW TESTAMENT MINISTRY AND MINISTERS

Scripture Reading: Acts 1:17, 25; 2 Cor. 4:1; 3:8-9; Eph. 3:8; Gal.1:6-9; Eph. 3:6-7; Col. 1:24-25; Eph. 4:11-12

Thus far, we have seen that in God's economy there is one goal and that God has ordained one way to reach this goal. Furthermore, to have the one way for the one goal we must be in the teaching and fellowship of the apostles. One way for one goal cannot be seen in today's Christianity because they are not in the sphere of the apostles' teaching and fellowship. There are many different teachings in today's Christianity. All these different teachings bring people into different fellowships, and the different fellowships are divisions in confusion. In the Lord's recovery, we have been brought to the one way for the one goal according to the teaching of the apostles to be in the unique fellowship of the apostles. The preserving factor of our being kept in one way for one goal is the apostles' teaching and fellowship. If we remain, live, and have our being in the apostles' teaching and fellowship, we can have one way for one goal. Otherwise, we will be misled into a divisive situation and have no sensation that we are in something wrong. We can serve God according to His New Testament economy only by taking the teaching of the apostles and by remaining in the fellowship of the apostles.

THE UNIQUE MINISTRY

In this chapter we want to fellowship concerning the New Testament ministry and ministers. The ministry of the New Testament economy is singular and unique, but the ministers of the New Testament economy are plural. In January of 1937 Brother Nee gave a series of messages on the church life in which he told us that all the gifted ones, such as the apostles, prophets, evangelists, shepherds and teachers, were given by the Head to the Body for the work of *the* ministry. He spoke strongly concerning the work of *the* ministry. In 1969 I was invited to a certain locality where the responsible brother stressed that he accepted all ministries. I enumerated some different "ministries" and asked him if he could receive them. He was forced to say that he accepted all ministries selectively. Although he would not say it, this was an admission that he did not receive all ministries. Even the denominations in Christianity do not receive all ministries. The Southern Baptists could never accept the ministry of the Presbyterians, while the Presbyterians could never accept the ministries of the Episcopalians or Lutherans. Neither would the Roman Catholic Church accept the ministries of the Protestant denominations.

As the recovery is increasing and spreading because of the new way to visit people by knocking on their doors to get them to believe and be baptized, the door is wide open for different opinions and different teachings. Some may ask how our present situation can be managed. From the very beginning of the recovery the Lord has shown and instructed us not to control the saints. Thank the Lord that we have never controlled the saints through the years. I can testify that in all the years I was with Brother Nee, he never controlled anyone. I hate control. I gave three elders' trainings from 1984 through 1986, in which I charged the elders repeatedly not to control others. To control others is ugly. To control others is not a glory, but a great shame.

Some may wonder, "Since we don't exercise control, won't there be confusion?" We must always remember the Lord's word in Proverbs 29:18: "Without a vision the people cast off restraint" (ASV). We need a clear vision. Man should not control, but the vision of God's New Testament economy should exercise control over each one of us. We all have to be under the control of the revelation of God's New Testament economy.

God has an economy to accomplish something for His

THE NEW TESTAMENT MINISTRY AND MINISTERS 161

eternal plan. God revealed His economy to His chosen ones such as Peter, John, James, Paul, and others who were working with Paul. These apostles and prophets received a commission from God. God charged them with a commission, and this commission is the ministry. The ministry is God's commission both in the Old and the New Testaments. In the Old Testament God came down to Mount Sinai and charged Moses with His commission to decree the law. That commission, the ministry of the law, was the ministry of the Old Testament. The ministry of the law in the Old Testament was singular and unique. It was *the* ministry, not the ministries. In 2 Corinthians Paul calls the ministry of the Old Testament the ministry of letter (3:6) and the ministry of condemnation (3:9). From the time of Moses many taught the law. The teachers of the law and the prophets carried out the one ministry of the law in the Old Testament, not many ministries. In 2 Corinthians 3 Paul compared that ministry with the New Testament ministry. The ministry of the law was singular and unique and the New Testament ministry is also singular and unique. The ministry of the law was the ministry of condemnation, while the New Testament ministry is the ministry of the Spirit and the ministry of righteousness (justification).

When the Lord Jesus was on this earth, He chose twelve apostles and gave them a commission, which was the ministry. In Acts 1 Peter refers to the commission the Lord gave them as "this ministry" (vv. 17, 25). Though the Apostles were twelve in number, their ministry was uniquely one. All the Apostles carried out the same ministry to bear the testimony not of any religion, doctrine, or practice, but uniquely of the incarnated, resurrected, and ascended Jesus Christ, the Lord of all. The Apostles did not have twelve respective ministries, but they all had one ministry. In 2 Corinthians 4:1 Paul said, "Therefore, having this ministry, as we have received mercy we do not lose heart." Paul and his co-workers, the apostles of Christ, had one unique ministry—the ministry of the new covenant for the accomplishment of God's New

Testament economy. In recent years the Lord has made the matter of the unique New Testament ministry very clear to us (see *Elders' Training—Book One—The Ministry of the New Testament*). In the New Testament economy of God there is only one ministry. Paul tells us in Ephesians 4:11-12 that even the perfected and equipped saints, not only the gifted persons like the apostles, prophets, evangelists, and shepherds and teachers, do the work of the ministry. The gifted ones perfect all the saints to do the work of the ministry that they are doing. We all are doing one work. Although there are millions of members of Christ, we all are doing the unique work of the ministry. The many members do not bear their own ministry. There are many ministries in today's degraded Christianity, but there are not many ministries in the New Testament. There is only one, unique New Testament ministry.

The ministry is to minister the very essence, the very substance, of God's New Testament economy. The New Testament ministry works to minister the very substance of God's New Testament economy into people's spirit, and this ministry is the ministry of the Spirit, the ministry of justification, and the ministry of life. This ministry is unique. You cannot say that you have a ministry different from the ministry Paul had. If you do have a ministry different from the Apostle Paul, your ministry will result in division. If each of us had different ministries, this would mean that we were building something of ourselves for ourselves. These different ministries would cause many divisions. In today's Christianity different ministries become divisions.

THE DANGER OF DIFFERENT MINISTRIES

The danger of different ministries can be seen in the inner life movement. The inner life movement began in the seventeenth century with the mystics in the Catholic Church such as Madam Guyon and Father Fenelon. William Law was raised up to express the teachings of the mystics in a more practical way. His teachings were a great help to Andrew Murray, who played a prominent role

THE NEW TESTAMENT MINISTRY AND MINISTERS 163

in recovering the truth concerning Christ as the believers' inward life and experience. Jesse Penn-Lewis received help from Andrew Murray and went on to see much concerning the subjective death of Christ. Her teachings were published in a paper called *The Overcomer*. Her teaching on the subjective death of Christ was very good. From the subjective death of Christ she went on to talk about spiritual warfare in a book entitled *War on the Saints*. Eventually, however, Mrs. Penn-Lewis went to an extreme on the matter of spiritual warfare, and at the end of her life, she became preoccupied with demons.

Late in Mrs. Penn-Lewis's ministry, T. Austin-Sparks was raised up. During a visit to Taiwan in 1955, Brother Sparks told me that when he was young, he was working with Mrs. Penn-Lewis. But at a certain point, he realized that he could not work with her anymore because as a sister she exercised too much headship. She took too much of a leadership role as the head. Brother Sparks left her to begin another work which became his own ministry. Some said that Mrs. Penn-Lewis had a very good ministry on the subjective death of Christ and that Brother Sparks had a very good ministry on the principles of Christ's resurrection life. Eventually, Mrs. Penn-Lewis went to be with the Lord, but her paper, *The Overcomer*, continued to be published. Brother Sparks also published a paper entitled *The Witness and the Testimony*. These two papers were in competition with one another. Sister Penn-Lewis and Brother Sparks had two ministries to produce two results of the work.

In our early days in the recovery, we read their writings and received much help from them. Both of them knew the Bible well and had spiritual insight. I received a great deal of help from one book written by Brother Sparks entitled *The Release of the Lord*. This book helped me to know the truth concerning the release of the incarnated Jesus in John 12:24, that is, that the one grain was released to be many grains. These dear saints, however, made a great mistake by keeping two different kinds of ministries. For two different ministries to be carried out by two ministers is altogether against the principle of the New Testament. The ministries of Sister Penn-Lewis and Brother Sparks became two kinds of works to produce two groups of people. One group followed Sister Penn-Lewis, and another group followed Brother Sparks. We must be warned by history so we do not repeat the mistakes made in the past. In the Lord's recovery there is only one ministry. If you say that the ministry is my ministry, you must say it with the realization that what I minister is the New Testament ministry. The New Testament ministry was commissioned by the Lord Jesus to His twelve Apostles and then to Paul and his co-workers. Brother Nee had a clear realization that there was only one ministry. The ministry of God's economy in the New Testament is uniquely one. All the serving ones, the ministers, should participate in the same ministry.

THE NEW TESTAMENT MINISTRY ACCORDING TO THE APOSTLES' TEACHING

The deciding factor in determining the right ministry, which is the ministry of God's New Testament economy, is the teaching of the apostles. A person's work is in the New Testament ministry if he teaches the teaching of the apostles. If he does not teach you according to the teaching of the apostles, his work is not participating in the ministry of the New Testament economy. The unique ministry is the ministry ordained by God according to the apostles' teaching.

The New Testament ministry, the unique ministry, the ministry of the Spirit and the ministry of righteousness (justification), is to bear the testimony of Jesus and to minister the processed and completed Christ to His believers according to the apostles' teaching (Eph. 3:8; Gal. 1:6-9). To preach anything other than the apostles' teaching is to preach something that is not a part of the ministry of the New Testament economy. This is why Paul charged the Galatians to discern those who pervert the gospel of Christ. A gospel other than the gospel that Paul preached to the Galatian believers is not the gospel (vv. 6-9). In other words, a gospel different from Paul's gospel is not in the New Testament ministry. We should not receive a gospel different from Paul's gospel, different from Paul's ministry. The ministry is unique in the teaching of the apostles.

THE NEW TESTAMENT MINISTERS

The New Testament ministers (2 Cor. 3:6) are the ministers of the gospel of Jesus Christ (Eph. 3:6-7). Whoever ministers the gospel of Jesus Christ as the Son of God becoming a man, dying on the cross for our sins, and resurrecting to impart life into us, is one of the New Testament ministers. These ministers are for the building up of the church (Col. 1:24-25). They are many, yet they have one unique ministry for the building up of the Body of Christ. All the ministers' different works should be for this unique ministry (Eph. 4:11-12).

Not only the gifted members but also the perfected saints are working the work of the ministry. It should not be that only a few are in the ministry, but all of us need to be in the ministry. When we go out to visit others, we need to speak the ministry. There is one ministry with thousands of ministers. In Christianity there are a few big speakers, but in the Lord's recovery we need to have thousands of speakers. These thousands of speakers should be ministers in the one ministry. The ministry is not merely the ministry of a few gifted ones, but it is the ministry of each one of the saints. It is the ministry of thousands of small ministers. The one ministry must be our ministry.

CHAPTER NINETEEN

THE LEADERSHIP IN THE NEW TESTAMENT MINISTRY AND AMONG THE NEW TESTAMENT MINISTERS

Scripture Reading: Acts 1:17, 25; Eph. 4:3-6; 1 Tim. 1:3-4; 6:3-5; 2 John 9-11

ONE UNIQUE LEADERSHIP

In the New Testament there is only one ministry and only one leadership in the ministry. Although there is the truth of the leadership in the New Testament ministry, the Lord did not officially appoint someone to be the leader. The early part of Acts shows us that Peter was taking the lead among the apostles (cf. Acts 1:15; 2:14). However, the Lord Jesus did not appoint Peter to be an official leader. The leadership was something spontaneous according to life, according to the real need, and according to the situation. A leadership is shaped by the growth in life and is an issue of the need. If there is no need, no leadership can be manifested. The environment forms and constitutes the leadership.

There is one unique leadership since the ministry is one (Acts 1:17, 25). Because the ministry is one, there should never be more than one leadership. There is also one unique leadership since God, the Lord, and the Spirit all are one (Eph. 4:4-6). Since there is one God, one Lord, and one Spirit, how could there be more than one leadership? The one unique leadership is for keeping the oneness of the Spirit for the Body of Christ (Eph. 4:3). Today's Christianity is divided because there are too many leaderships. Every leader has a group which is the sphere of his leadership, and that sphere becomes a division. Thus, if the matter of leadership is not applied or viewed properly, it will create division.

THE LEADERSHIP IN THE APOSTLES' TEACHING

The leadership is produced, strengthened, and also limited, restricted, in the apostles' teaching. In 1 Timothy 1:3-4 Paul charged Timothy to remain in Ephesus to do one thing with a definite purpose. He was there to charge the dissenting ones not to teach the things different from the economy of God in faith. He had to charge these ones not to teach things that were different from the apostles' teaching, which is concerning God's New Testament economy to dispense the processed Triune God into His chosen and redeemed people that Christ might have a Body to express Himself and that the Triune God might have a complete, eternal expression in the New Jerusalem. Any minister who preaches or teaches should carry out such a ministry. Otherwise, this preacher or this minister should be limited. Paul had the authority to charge people not to teach differently from God's economy. Timothy was to tell these dissenting ones that their way of teaching had to be restricted and corrected. First Timothy shows us that there was some leadership that charged people to teach the right thing.

We can also see the leadership in the apostles' teaching in 2 John 9-11 where John charges the believers not to receive those who go beyond the teaching of Christ. To go beyond the teaching of Christ is to go beyond the teaching of the apostles. Second John 10-11 says, "If anyone comes to you and does not bring this teaching, do not receive him into your house, and do not say to him, Rejoice! For he who says to him, Rejoice, shares in his evil works." John's charge prohibits the believers from receiving these kinds of ministers. To say "Rejoice" to someone was used for greeting. The believers were not even to greet those who came to them and did not bring the teaching of Christ. Such a strong charge indicates the leadership in the New Testament ministry.

Paul, in his work in the New Testament ministry, exercised leadership to correct those who taught wrongly, and John exercised his leadership to charge the believers not to receive those who taught heresy, which was not

THE LEADERSHIP IN THE NEW TESTAMENT 169

according to the teaching of the apostles. The apostles who participated in the ministry of the New Testament economy did exercise some leadership.

NOT THE LEADERSHIP IN ORGANIZATION

Such a leadership as exercised by Paul and by John was not the leadership in organization. The first twelve Apostles were appointed by the Lord Jesus, but they were not organized. The Lord Jesus' appointment was equal among the twelve. In the New Testament we cannot see an organization with board members, a chairman, a secretary, or other officers. All the major denominations have board members and a chairman. The Catholic Church has the pope as the head of their hierarchical organization. But the leadership in the New Testament ministry is not the leadership in the worldly sense to control others. In the Lord's recovery we do not have board members with a chairman or president.

Furthermore, this leadership is not the leadership in the ministers' acts, but in their teaching to restrict them from being divisive. Sometimes in the New Testament Paul told some of his co-workers to go to certain places (1 Cor. 4:17) or to remain in other places (Titus 1:5). But basically speaking, the leadership is not exercised over the ministers' acts. No one should exercise any control over the work for the Lord. If one has the burden to go to Alaska, he must be clear that this is of the Lord. No one controls his going or not going, but he needs to be clear that his decision is of the Lord through fellowship with the Lord and the Body. There is no restriction exercised in the movements of the workers, but if someone rises up to teach something beyond the teaching of the apostles, the leadership may rise up to tell this one not to teach differently. The leadership which is shown in the New Testament is mainly in the teachings of the ministers, not in the acts of co-workers.

As the Lord's recovery is spreading throughout the entire world, who can direct the acts of so many co-workers and serving ones? We do not have a board or a mission to direct the acts of the co-workers. No one is in a position to direct the ministers' acts. They must pray and seek the Lord's leading and fellowship with the dear saints who are so concerned for the Lord's move on this earth today. Through fellowship and prayer with the saints, they will be clear whether they should stay where they are or go to another place. They will be clear whether they should go by themselves or go with some others. What is taught or preached by the workers, however, should be restricted. The leadership is very much needed in this area.

In the recovery in God's ministry, there is no freedom to preach whatever we like to preach or to teach whatever we like to teach. Our preaching and our teaching have to be restricted under the leadership by the revelation of God's New Testament economy. If someone in the Lord's recovery began to teach, stress, or promote something contrary to or different from God's New Testament economy, there would be the need of some leadership to restrict this. Then there would be no confusion. There would never be confusion in the Lord's recovery if all of us had a clear revelation of the ministry in God's New Testament economy.

In the past, the Lord's recovery was disturbed by some who stressed the matter of tongue-speaking. The majority of Christians have still not accepted the matter of speaking in tongues, and in actuality this matter has done much damage to the Lord's move on this earth. With the matter of speaking in tongues, the debit is much bigger than the credit. In the early years of the Lord's recovery on mainland China we suffered a great loss when we tried to practice speaking in tongues. Eventually the co-workers there spontaneously concluded that tongue-speaking was not a profit to the Lord's move on this earth.

A certain charismatic magazine printed an article in which the writer said that he had contacted two hundred people who claimed to speak in tongues. Without exception, all of these two hundred doubted that the tongue spoken was genuine. However, the writer encouraged them all to go on speaking in tongues regardless of their doubts about the genuineness of what they were uttering. We read this article publicly in the training in 1963. Then I asked the trainees if Peter and the others on the day of Pentecost had any doubt whether the tongues spoken by them were genuine. Certainly Peter and the others had no such doubts. However, these two hundred tongue-speakers had doubts because the tongues they spoke were not genuine.

Furthermore, in 1963 and 1964 there were newspaper reports about some Pentecostal prophecies that an earthquake would strike the city of Los Angeles and that the city would fall into the ocean. However, the date of the predicted earthquake passed, and nothing happened. Certainly this lack of fulfillment is sufficient to prove that this prophecy was a falsehood. For a number of years, we in the Lord's recovery in China were under the influence of the Pentecostal things. Through our experience we can testify that our involvement with Pentecostalism was more of a loss than a gain. The greatest damage of Pentecostalism is that it makes it difficult for believers to appreciate the inward organic union with the Triune God. Many believers are interested in speaking in tongues, healing, and miracles, but not in the development and cultivation of the organic union with the Triune God.

From the very beginning of the Lord's recovery in the United States, I told the saints that I believed there was the matter of speaking in tongues in the Bible, but according to our observation and experience, the speaking in tongues in today's charismatic movement is not genuine, but is humanly manufactured. Some say that they can teach others to speak in tongues. They do this by encouraging others to speak in nonsense syllables. Obviously, this "speaking in tongues" is not a genuine dialect. To speak in tongues in this way does not minister life and does not build up the believers. When some were stressing speaking in tongues in the Lord's recovery, this created a problem. I did not give any orders to prohibit this, but I did my best to have a thorough fellowship with the saints to tell them that speaking in tongues does not minister life or help the Lord's recovery at all.

There is the danger of teachings coming in among us that stress things other than God's New Testament economy. We do not need to exercise too much leadership over these kinds of things, but we need to teach the saints in the Lord's recovery to learn the New Testament economy. By learning God's economy, the saints will have the ability to discern what is needed and what is not needed. The saints who have a vision of God's New Testament economy would not care for teachings that stress and emphasize other things. Because of the Lord's new way, the door is wide open for everyone to speak and to act. Therefore, we must be restricted by the heavenly vision, by the revelation of the New Testament economy.

THE LEADERSHIP IN ACTUALITY

The leadership in the New Testament ministry in actuality is not the leadership of one controlling person. In the Lord's recovery we reject the notion of one person controlling persons and matters. We do have some leadership, but not the leadership of one controlling person. Instead, we have the leadership of one controlling revelation in the one ministry through those who bring in the revelation of the ministry. The revelation controls, and it controls through those who bring in the revelation. The revelation in the Lord's recovery controls us and restricts us.

The ministry among us is not the ministry of a single person, but the unique New Testament ministry, the ministry of the Lord's move on this earth in the dispensation of the church. The Lord's move on this earth is through His unique ministry, and we are all participating in this unique ministry. Even our going out to visit people by knocking on their doors is a part of this unique ministry. The leadership is not the leadership of any single person who is controlling people in the Lord's recovery. The leadership in the Lord's recovery is the leadership of the God-given revelation that restricts us, directs us, and controls us so that confusion and division can be avoided.

Thank the Lord for the unique ministry and for the

unique leadership in this ministry. I am so happy that we all receive one revelation under one leadership, taking one way and reaching one goal. If all of the saints in the Lord's recovery would rise up to take the God-ordained way to practice the New Testament economy, what an impact we would have! In the Lord's new way, all the saints have many opportunities to serve the Lord by knocking on doors, baptizing people, setting up home meetings, teaching the truth, and helping people to grow in life. We must cooperate with the Lord to pick up the new way, the God-ordained way, to practice the New Testament economy. I do believe that this will bring back the Lord Jesus.